The Beatles

Das illustrierte Song Book

The Beatles

Das illustrierte Song Book

Herausgegeben von

Alan Aldridge

GOLDMANN VERLAG

Zuerst erschienen in zwei Bänden 1969 und 1971,
sowie 1980 bei Macdonald
1990 Neuausgabe in einem Band bei Macdonald & Co.
Die vorliegende Ausgabe erschien 1998
bei Little, Brown & Company, London

1. Auflage

Deutsche Texte von Peter Zentner und Lutz-W. Wolff.
Umschlaggestaltung: Design Team München nach einem Entwurf
von Andrew Barron & Collis Clements Associates
Abbildung auf der Umschlagrückseite: Peter Max
Abbildung auf der Titelseite: aus dem Artikel
The Beatles Sinister Songbook im *Observer,* November 1967
Satz + Lithographie: Lorenz & Zeller, Inning a. Ammersee
Druck und Bindung: MOHN Media GmbH, Gütersloh
Printed in Germany 2000
ISBN 3-442-30932-8
www.goldmann-verlag.de

Allen gewidmet,

die's nicht verstehen konnten,
und Rita, Miles und Saffron,
die es schafften.

Patrick

Vorwort

Gibt es einen Superlativ, mit dem die Beatles noch nicht beschrieben worden sind?

Der Einfluss der Beatles auf die Popmusik der sechziger Jahre, als dieses Buch erstmals in zwei Bänden veröffentlicht wurde, war enorm. Und er dauert an. Ihre Kompositionen, ihre Alben und selbst ihre Filme haben die moderne Unterhaltungsindustrie geprägt, und werden es auch weiterhin tun – auch wenn die noch lebenden ehemaligen Band-Mitglieder seit langem eigene Wege gehen und weder gemeinsam auftreten noch gemeinsam komponieren oder Aufnahmen machen.

Alan Aldridges Einleitung zum ersten Band geht dem Mythos Beatles einst und jetzt nach. Sein Buch, von dem er sich wünschte, dass es die Sinne und die Fantasie ebenso anregen möge wie ein Album der Beatles, erfüllt diesen Anspruch auch heute noch.

Mit der Ermordung John Lennons im Dezember 1980 wurden die Träume von der Wiedervereinigung der »Fab Four« für alle Zeit zerschlagen. Dieses Buch, das Beiträge einiger der größten Künstler unserer Zeit enthält, ist mehr als die Abbildung des Stils eines vergangenen Jahrzehnts, es ist eine Hommage an eine Zeit und ihre wohl herausragendsten Musiker. Die Faszination ist ungebrochen und Spaß für alle ist garantiert.

Zur Entstehung des Buches

Es ist beinah respektlos, die Beatles durch eine irdische Brille zu betrachten – als die Popgruppe etwa, die sich zur größten Rock'n'Roll-Attraktion aller Zeiten mauserte. Während ihre frühen Auftritte beispiellose Szenen der Massenhysterie heraufbeschworen, entwickelte sich ihre Musik im Laufe der Jahre zu einer faszinierenden Sozialgeschichte unserer Generation und ihrer Kultur. Die Beatles haben den Pop aus der Taufe gehoben: Pop als Musik und als Lebensstil. Diese Tatsache war es, die mich auf den Gedanken brachte, dieses Buch herauszubringen.

Der Tiefgang der Liedertexte der Beatles wurde mir 1967 zum ersten Mal bewusst. Es war während Sergeant Peppers Zeit, und ich besuchte eine Party. Lucy in the Sky with Diamonds, so flüsterte mir jemand ins Ohr, sei ein Lied über einen LSD-Trip. Nun, Vieldeutigkeit in Schlagertexten war nichts Neues – doch die vielen Interpretationen der Songs auf dem Sergeant-Pepper-Album fesselten mich so sehr, dass ich damit begann, alle Liedertexte der Beatles zu lesen und allen möglichen versteckten Bedeutungen nachzuspüren. Eine Zeile aus Eleanor Rigby sprang mir besonders ins Auge: »Trägt das Gesicht, das sie sonst in den Krug vor dem Tor legt.« Surrealismus pur, fand ich. Da dies auch das Feld war, das ich als Zeichner bestellte, beschloss ich in meiner kindlichen Arglosigkeit, den Autor der Zeile zu interviewen, Paul McCartney. Das führte zu einem Aufsatz, der eine wahre Flut von Fanpost auslöste, als er zusammen mit meinen Zeichnungen veröffentlicht wurde. Von da an war's nur ein kleiner Schritt, und ich machte mich an die Vorarbeiten zu diesem Buch, das die besten Texte der Beatles enthält.

Rund 200 Beatles-Songs wurden bisher veröffentlicht. Doch viele der frühen Kompositionen sind thematisch nicht sehr abwechslungsreich. Sie boten zu wenig Kontrast in illustratorischer Hinsicht, und wir konnten uns leichten Herzens von ihnen trennen. Unsere 43 Mitarbeiter erhielten Listen, auf denen sie die Lieder ankreuzen sollten, die sie illustrieren wollten. Es dauerte nicht lang, und beinah alle Songs, die ich mir vornehmen wollte, befanden sich in anderen guten Händen. So ist das Leben.

Dieses Buch soll die Sinne und die Fantasie anregen wie es die Musik der Beatles tut. Einen Text zu illustrieren, ist für jeden Künstler eine Herausforderung. Was wir hier getan haben, steht in einer langen Tradition. Immer schon haben Künstler Gedichte und Texte der Bibel illustriert. Und in gewissem Sinn sind die Beatles Religion: Was sie sagen und was sie sind inspiriert uns alle.

Ich sehe in der Musik und den Texten der Beatles ein ungeheures Sprungbrett in die Fantasie. Sie sind einzigartig in ihrem Reiz und ihrer Vielfalt – eine Palette, von der wohl jeder Maler träumt.

Die Texte haben den Künstlern als Katalysator zur Umsetzung ihrer Ideen gedient. Manche der Illustrationen sind sehr fantasievoll, andere dagegen erscheinen simpel. Doch meistens nur auf den ersten Blick. Der Freiheit der Interpretation sind keine Grenzen gesetzt.

Dieses Buch soll mehr sein als nur eine Sammlung illustrierter Songs der Beatles. In meinen Augen ist es ein Porträt der sechziger Jahre.

Auch die Fans haben wir aufgerufen, uns ihre kreativen Beiträge zuzuschicken. Zärtlich gehütete Werke wurden uns in Massen zugesandt, von zwei Meter hohen Ölgemälden bis hin zu winzigen Bleistiftzeichnungen, die John und Yoko darstellen. Wir erhielten auch zahlreiche Schmähbriefe, was mich eher überraschte. Na schön, das muss wohl sein. Wo viel Licht, da auch viel Schatten.

Die Beatles und ihre Musik haben das Tempo der Welt von heute eingefangen. Was sie zum Stil ihrer Generation beigetragen haben, wollen wir mit diesem Buch festhalten.

Alan Aldridge, 1969

I

Beatlemania
1962 → 1965

I saw her standing there

Well, she was just seventeen,
You know what I mean,
And the way she looked was way beyond compare,
So how could I dance with another,
oh when I saw her standing there.
Well she looked at me,
and I, I could see,
that before too long I'd fall in love with her,
she wouldn't dance with another,
oh when I saw her dancing there.
Well my heart went zoom when I crossed that room,
and I held her hand in mine.
Oh we danced through the night,
and we held each other tight,
and before too long I fell in love with her,
now I'll never dance with another,
oh when I saw her standing there.
Well my heart went zoom when I crossed that room,
and I held her hand in mine.
Oh we danced through the night,
and we held each other tight,
and before too long I fell in love with her,
now I'll never dance with another,
oh since I saw her standing there.
Oh since I saw her standing there.

Misery

The world is treating me bad, misery.
I'm the kind of guy who never used to cry,
The world is treating me bad, misery.
I've lost her now for sure,
I won't see her no more,
It's gonna be a drag, misery.
I'll remember all the little things we've done,
Can't she see she'll be the only one, lonely one,
Send her back to me 'cos ev'ry one can see,
Without her I will be in misery.
I'll remember all the little things we've done,
She'll remember and she'll be the only
one, lonely one,
Send her back to me 'cos ev'ry one can see,
Without her I will be in misery.
Oo in misery. Oo in misery.

Ask me why

I love you,
Can't you tell me things I want to know?
And it's true that it really only goes to show
That I know that I I I I should never, never, never be blue.
Now you're mine,
My happiness still makes me cry.
And in time you'll understand the reason why
If I cry it's not because I'm sad
But you're the only love that I've ever had.
I can't believe it's happened to me.
I can't conceive of any more misery.
Ask me why
I'll say I love you and I'm always thinking of you.

Please please me

Last night I said these words to my girl
I know you never even try girl
Come on, come on, come on, come on,
Please please me oh Yeh like I please you.
You don't need me to show the way love
Why do I always have to say love
Come on, come on, come on, come on,
Please please me oh Yeh like I please you.
I don't want to sound complaining
But you know there's always rain in my heart.
I do all the pleasing with you
It's so hard to reason with you.
Oh yeh why do you make me blue.
Last night I said these words to my girl,
I know you never even try girl,
Come on, come on, come on, come on
Please please me oh Yeh like I please you – you.

Love me do

Love, love me do,
you know I love you.
I'll always be true
so please love me do, who ho love me do.
Love, love me do,
you know I love you.
I'll always be true
so please love me do, who ho love me do.
Someone to love, somebody new.
Someone to love, someone like you.
Love, love me do,
you know I love you.
I'll always be true
so please love me do, who ho love me do.
Love, love me do,
you know I love you
I'll always be true
so please love me do, who ho love me do.

›Dahin möchten wir wieder zurück – zur Einfachheit. Es gibt nichts Einfacheres als ›Komm, hab mich lieb‹. Das heißt es eben. Ich hab damals die Schule geschwänzt, glaub ich, um mit John dieses Lied zu schreiben, als wir anfingen.‹

Paul

PS I love you

As I write this letter, send my love to you,
remember that I'll always be in love with you.
Treasure these few words till we're together
keep all my love forever.
PS I love you, you, you, you.
I'll be coming home again to you love,
until the day I do love.
PS I love you, you, you, you.
As I write this letter, send my love to you,
remember that I'll always be in love with you.
Treasure these few words till we're together
keep all my love forever.
PS I love you, you, you, you.
As I write this letter, send my love to you,
(you know I want you to)
remember that I'll always be in love with you.
I'll be coming home again to you love,
until the day I do love.
PS I love you, you, you, you,
I love you.

›In den ersten zwei, zweieinhalb Jahren hatte ich noch nicht das Gefühl dazuzugehören. Sie waren die Beatles und ich war der neue Schlagzeuger. Das dauerte lange genug, um mich zu ärgern. Aber jetzt ist es vorbei.‹

Ringo

Do you want to know a secret?

You'll never know how much I really love you,
You'll never know how much I really care,

Listen, do you want to know a secret,
Do you promise not to tell, Whoa .....
Closer let me whisper in your ear,
Say the words you long to hear,
I'm in love with you, oo .....

I've known the secret for a week or two,
Nobody knows just we two.

Listen, do you want to know a secret,
Do you promise not to tell, Whoa .....
Closer let me whisper in your ear,
Say the words you long to hear,
I'm in love with you, oo, oo, oo, oo .....

There's a place

There, there's a place,
Where I can go,
When I feel low,
When I feel blue,
And it's my mind,
And there's no time,
When I'm alone.
I think of you,
And things you do,
Go round my head,
The things you've said,
Like I love only you.
In my mind there's no sorrow,
Don't you know that it's so,
There'll be no sad tomorrow,
Don't you know that it's so.
There, there's a place,
Where I can go,
When I feel low,
When I feel blue,
And it's my mind,
And there's no time,
When I'm alone.
There, there's a place,
There's a place.

‘Genau wie in
Butlins Ferienlager.’
Ringo
bei seiner Rückkehr
vom Meditieren
im Rishikesh im
Himalaya

From me to you

If there's anything that you want,
if there's anything I can do,
just call on me and I'll send it along,
with love from me to you.
I've got ev'rything that you want,
like a heart that's oh so true,
just call on me and I'll send it along,
with love from me to you.
I got arms that long to hold you,
and keep you by my side,
I got lips that long to kiss you,
and keep you satisfied.
If there's anything that you want,
if there's anything I can do,
just call on me and I'll send it along,
with love from me to you.
Just call on me and I'll send it along,
with love from me you.
I got arms that long to hold you,
and keep you by my side,
I got lips that long to kiss you,
and keep you satisfied.
If there's anything that you want,
if there's anything I can do,
just call on me and I'll send it along,
with love from me to you.

"Das haben Paul und ich geschrieben, als wir auf Tour waren. Beinahe hätten wir's gar nicht aufgenommen. Wir dachten, es wäre zu Blues-mäßig, aber als wir's fertig hatten und George Martin die Mundharmonika unterlegt hatte, war es in Ordnung."
John

Thank you girl

Oh, oh
you've been good to me, you made me glad when I was blue,
and eternally I'll always be in love with you,
and all I gotta do is thank you girl, thank you girl.
I could tell the world, a thing or two about our love,
I know little girl, only a fool would doubt our love,
and all I gotta do is thank you girl, thank you girl.
Thank you girl for loving me the way that you do,
(way that you do),
that's the kind of love that is too good to be true,
and all I gotta do is thank you girl, thank you girl.
Oh, oh,
you've been good to me, you made me glad when I was blue,
and eternally I'll always be in love with you,
and all I gotta do is thank you girl, thank you girl.
Oh, oh.

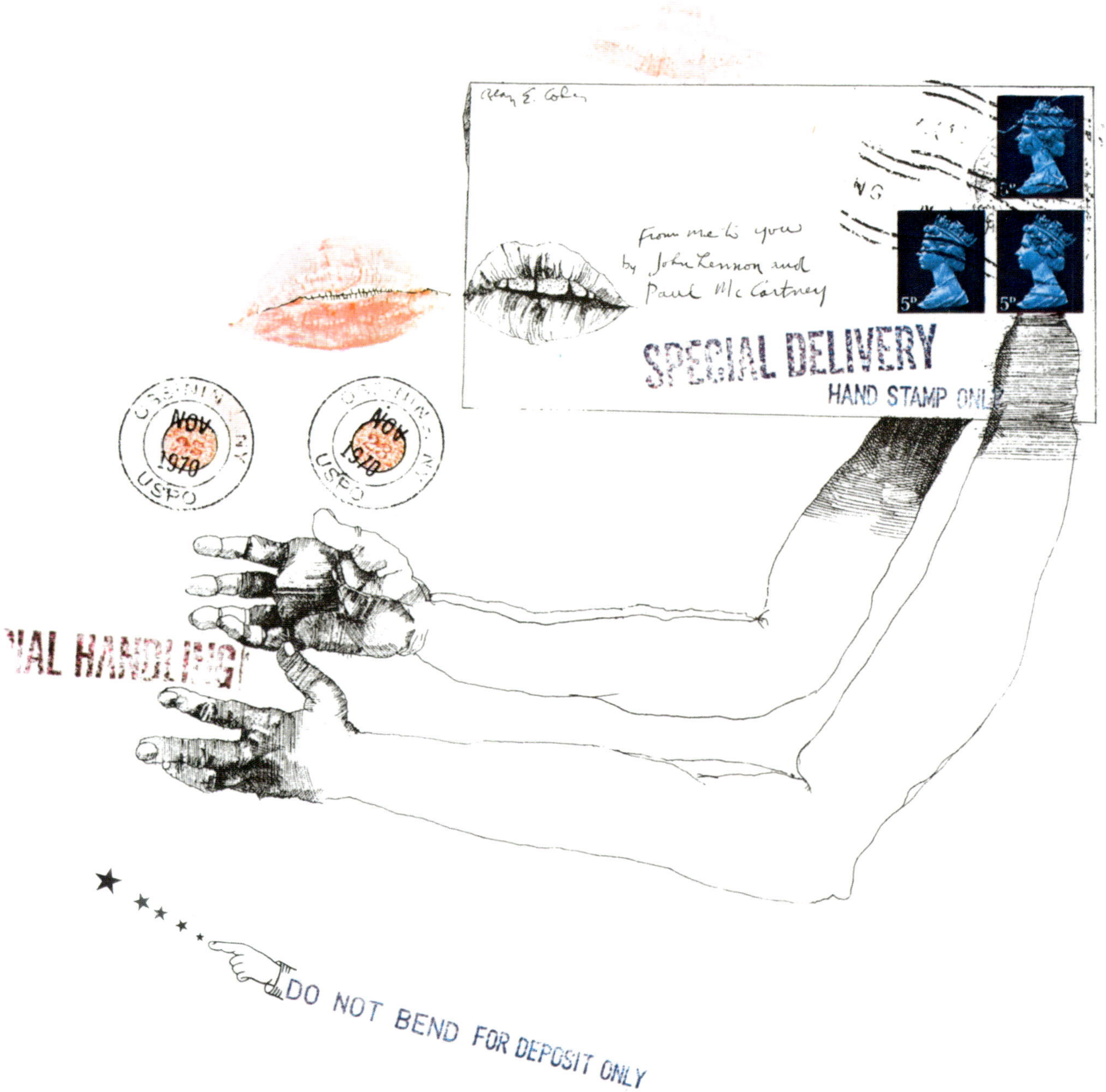
From me to you
by John Lennon and
Paul McCartney
SPECIAL DELIVERY
HAND STAMP ONLY
NOV
1970
USPO
AL HANDLING
DO NOT BEND FOR DEPOSIT ONLY

Spanfeller

I'll be on my way

The sun is fading away.
That's the end of the day.
As the June-light
turns to moonlight
I'll be on my way.
Just one kiss then I'll go.
Don't hide the tears that don't show.
As the June-light
turns to moonlight
I'll be on my way.
To where the winds don't blow
and golden rivers flow,
this way I will go.
They were right, I was wrong,
true love didn't last long.
As the June-light
turns to moonlight
I'll be on my way.
To where the winds don't blow
and golden rivers flow,
this way I will go.
They were right, I was wrong,
true love didn't last long.
As the June-light
turns to moonlight
I'll be on my way.

Released by Billy J Kramer and
the Dakotas, April 1963

„Der Zirkus hat die Stadt zwar verlassen, aber das Grundstück gehört uns noch immer."
John

Tip of my tongue

When I want to speak to you,
it sometimes takes a week or two
to think of things I want to say to you,
but words just stay on the tip of my tongue.
When the skies are not so blue,
there's nothing left for me to do
just think of something new to say to you,
but words just stay on the tip of my tongue.
People say I'm lonely,
only know that's not true.
You know I'm waiting for a chance
to prove my love to you.
Soon enough my time will come,
and after all is said and done
I'll marry you and we will live as one,
with no more words on the tip of my tongue no more,
no words on the tip of my tongue.

Released by Tommy Quickly, July 1963

„Als ich ungefähr zwölf war, dachte ich, dass ich ein Genie wäre und dass es bloß noch keiner gemerkt hätte. Wenn es tätsächlich Genies gibt, dann bin ich wohl eins, aber wenn es keine gibt, ist es mir auch egal."
John

Bad to me

If you ever leave me, I'll be sad and blue,
don't you ever leave me, I'm so in love with you.
The birds in the sky would be sad and lonely,
if they knew that I'd lost my one and only,
they'd be sad, if you're bad to me.
The leaves on the trees would be softly sighin',
if they heard from the breeze that you left me cryin',
they'd be sad, don't be bad to me.
But I know you won't leave me 'cos you told me so,
and I've no intention of letting you go,
just as long as you let me know, you won't be bad to me.
So the birds in the sky won't be sad and lonely,
'cos they know that I got my one and only,
they'll be glad, you're not bad to me.
But I know you won't leave me 'cos you told me so,
and I've no intention of letting you go,
just as long as you let me know, you won't be bad to me.
So the birds in the sky won't be sad and lonely,
'cos they know that I got my one and only,
they'll be glad, you're not bad to me.

Released by Billy J Kramer and the Dakotas, April 1963

She loves you

She loves you yeh, yeh, yeh,
She loves you yeh, yeh, yeh.
You think you've lost your love,
Well I saw her yesterday – yi – yay,
It's you she's thinking of,
And she told me what to say – yi – yay,
She says she loves you,
and you know that can't be bad,
Yes, she loves you,
And you know you should be glad.
She said you hurt her so,
She almost lost her mind,
And now she says she knows,
You're not the hurting kind.
She says she loves you,
And you know that can't be bad,
Yes, she loves you,
And you know you should be glad.
She loves you yeh, yeh, yeh,
She loves you yeh, yeh, yeh.
And with a love like that,
You know you should be glad.
You know it's up to you,
I think it's only fair,
Pride can hurt you too,
Apologise to her.
Because she loves you,
And you know that can't be bad,
Yes, she loves you,
And you know you should be glad.
She loves you yeh, yeh, yeh,
She loves you yeh, yeh, yeh.
With a love like that,
You know you should be glad.
With a love like that,
You know you should be glad.
With a love like that,
You know you should be glad.
Yeh, yeh, yeh,
Yeh, yeh, yeh.

I'll get you

Oh yeh, oh yeh.
Imagine, I'm in love with you,
it's easy 'cos I know,
I've imagined I'm in love with you,
many, many, many times before.
It's not like me to pretend,
but I'll get you in the end,
yes I will, I'll get you in the end, oh yeh, oh yeh.
I think about you night and day,
I need you 'cos it's true.
When I think about you, I can say,
I'm never, never, never blue.
So I'm telling you, my friend,
that I'll get you, I'll get you in the end,
yes I will, I'll get you in the end, oh yeh, oh yeh.
Well, there's gonna be a time,
well I'm gonna change my mind.
So you might as well resign yourself to me, oh yeh.
Imagine, I'm in love with you,
it's easy 'cos I know,
I've imagined I'm in love with you,
many, many, many times before.
It's not like me to pretend,
but I'll get you in the end,
yes I will, I'll get you in the end, oh yeh, oh yeh.

„Wir streiten uns immer. Wir schreien und kreischen und heulen, und dann vertragen wir uns wieder, was immer sehr schön ist. Es ist, als wäre man der Psychiater des anderen. Wir behandeln uns gegenseitig."
Yoko

Kalish

„Ich fühle mich jünger werden. Sogar körperlich. Teils kommt das natürlich von meiner Ernährung: denn du weißt ja: man ist, was man isst. Aber es kommt auch daher, dass ich John begegnet bin."
Yoko

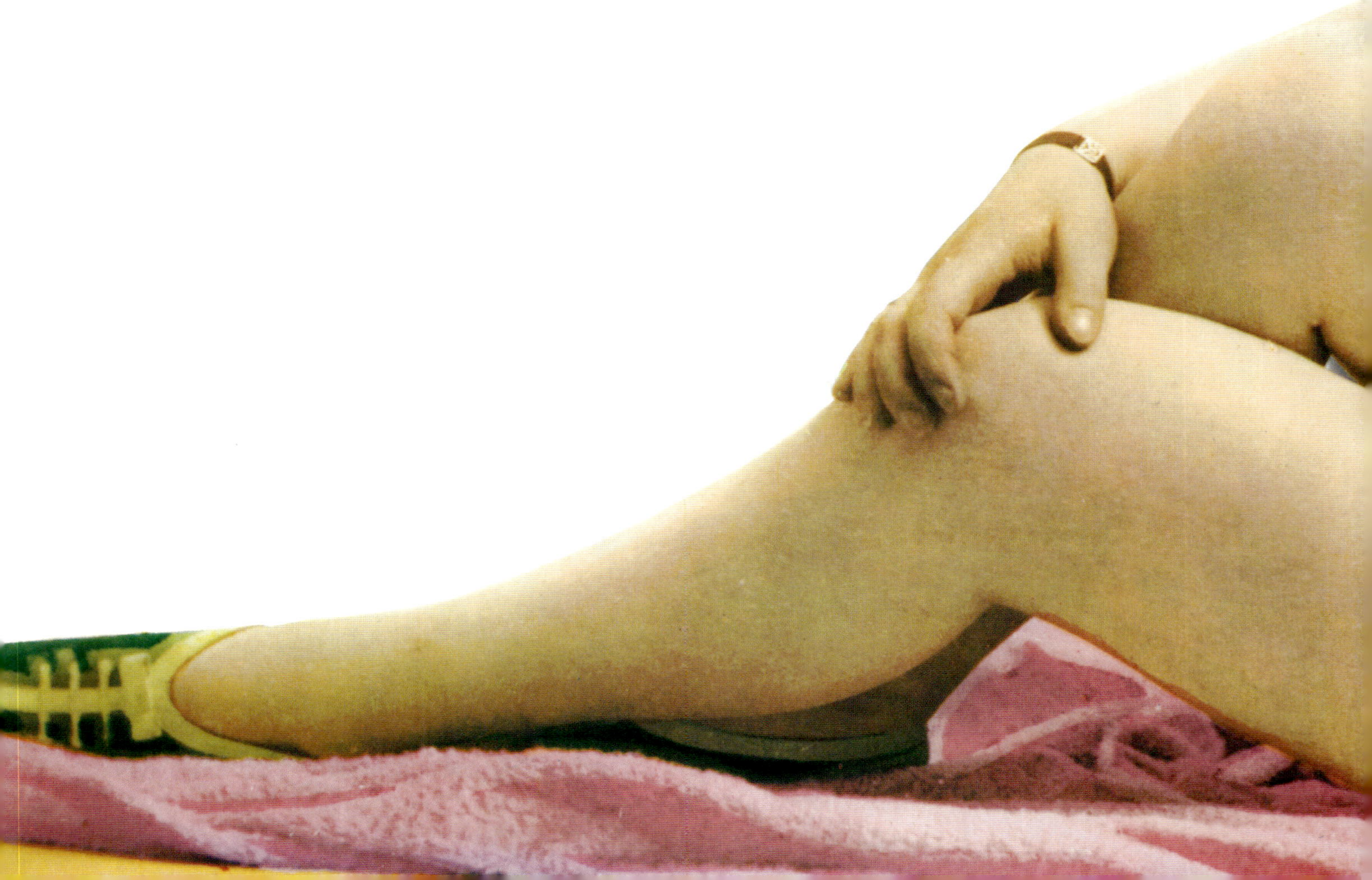

Love of the loved

Each time I look into your eyes,
I see that there the heaven lies,
and as I look I see the love of the loved.
Someday they'll see that from the start,
my place has been deep in your heart,
and in your heart I see the love of the loved.
Though I've said it all before,
I'll say it more and more,
now that I'm really sure you love me,
and I know that from today I'll see it in the way,
that you look at me and say you love me
So let it rain what do I care,
deep in your heart I'll still be there,
and when I'm there I see the love of the loved.
Though I've said it all before,
I'll say it more and more,
now that I'm really sure you love me,
and I know that from today, I'll see it in the way,
that you look at me and say you love me.
So let it rain, what do I care,
deep in your heart I'll still be there,
and when I'm there, I see the love of the loved,
I see the love of the loved.

Released by Cilla Black, September 1963

❛Dass John sich in Yoko verliebt hat, dafür kann man ihm doch keine Vorwürfe machen. Genauso wenig wie mir, weil ich mich in Linda verliebt habe. Am Anfang war ich eifersüchtig und wütend, und ich hatte Angst, dass unsere Partnerschaft kaputt gehen würde. Ich habe ein Jahr gebraucht, bis ich begriffen habe, dass die beiden sich lieben.❜
Paul

Ken Matsunaga

Hello little girl

When I see you ev'ry day, I say mm-mm,
hello little girl,
when you're passing on your way, I say
mm-mm, hello little girl.
If I see you passing by, I cry mm-mm,
hello little girl,
when I try to catch your eye, I cry
mm-mm, hello little girl.
I send you flowers, but you don't care,
you never seem to see me standing there.
I often wonder, what you're thinking of,
I hope it's me (love, love, love).
So I hope there'll come a day, when you'll
say mm-mm,
you're my girl.
When I see you ev'ry day, I say mm-mm,
hello little girl,
when you're passing on your way, I say
mm-mm, hello little girl.
It's not the first time, it's happened to me,
it's been a long, long time and it's so funny to see
that I'm about to lose my mind.
So I hope there'll come a day, when you'll
say mm-mm, you're my girl.
You're my little girl.

Released by Fourmost, October 1963

»Das ist eins der ersten Lieder, die ich je zu Ende geschrieben habe. Ich war damals achtzehn, und wir hatten es den Fourmost gegeben. Ich glaube, das war das erste eigene Lied, das ich versucht habe, mit der Gruppe zu machen.«
John

It won't be long

It won't be long yeh, yeh,
it won't be long yeh, yeh,
it won't be long yeh, yeh,
till I belong to you.
Ev'ry night when ev'rybody has fun,
here am I sitting all on my own.
It won't be long yeh, yeh,
it won't be long yeh, yeh,
it won't be long yeh, yeh,
till I belong to you.
Since you left me I'm so alone,
now you're coming, you're coming home,
I'll be good like I know I should,
you're coming home, you're coming home.
Ev'ry night the tears come down from my eyes,
ev'ry day I've done nothing but cry.
It won't be long yeh, yeh,
Since you left me I'm so alone,
now you're coming, you're coming home.
Ev'ry day we'll be happy, I know,
now I know that you won't leave me no more.
It won't be long yeh, yeh.

»Auch ein ganz frühes. Als ich meine Therapie in Kalifornien gemacht habe, wurde ich gezwungen, jedes Lied zu lesen, das ich geschrieben habe. Ich konnte selbst kaum glauben, wie viele es waren.«
John

All I've got to do

Whenever I want you around, yeh,
All I gotta do
Is call you on the phone
And you'll come running home,
Yeh, that's all I gotta do.
And when I wanna kiss you, yeh,
All I gotta do
Is whisper in your ear the words you want to hear,
And I'll be kissing you.
And the same goes for me whenever you want me at all,
I'll be here, yes I will, whenever you call,
You just gotta call on me, yeh, you just gotta call on me.
And when I wanna kiss you, yeh,
All I gotta do
Is call you on the phone
And you'll come running home,
Yeh, that's all I gotta do.
And the same goes for me whenever you want me at all,
I'll be here, yes I will, whenever you call,
You just gotta call on me, yeh, you just gotta call on me.

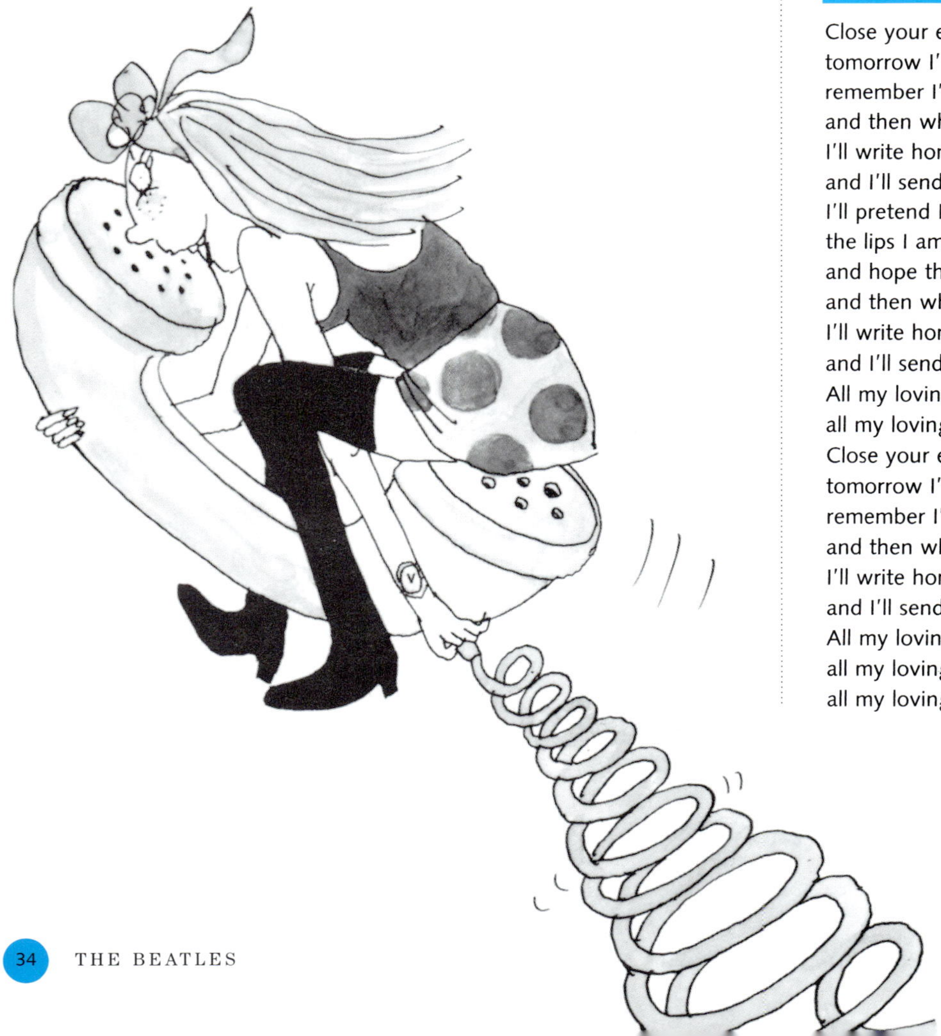

Little child

Little child, little child,
little child, won't you dance with me?
I'm so sad and lonely,
baby take a chance with me.
Little child, little child,
little child, won't you dance with me?
I'm so sad and lonely,
baby take a chance on me.
If you want someone to make you feel so fine
then we'll have some fun when you're mine, all mine,
so come on, come on, come on.
Little child, little child,
little child, won't you dance with me?
I'm so sad and lonely,
baby take a chance with me.
When you're by my side, you're the only one,
don't you run and hide, just come on, come on,
so come on, come on, come on.
Little child, little child,
little child, won't you dance with me?
I'm so sad and lonely,
baby take a chance with me.
Oh yeh, baby take a chance with me.

All my loving

Close your eyes and I'll kiss you,
tomorrow I'll miss you,
remember I'll always be true,
and then while I'm away,
I'll write home every day,
and I'll send all my loving to you.
I'll pretend I am kissing,
the lips I am missing,
and hope that my dreams will come true,
and then while I'm away,
I'll write home every day,
and I'll send all my loving to you.
All my loving, I will send to you,
all my loving, darling, I'll be true.
Close your eyes and I'll kiss you,
tomorrow I'll miss you,
remember I'll always be true,
and then while I'm away,
I'll write home every day,
and I'll send all my loving to you.
All my loving, I will send to you,
all my loving, darling, I'll be true,
all my loving, I will send to you.

Hold me tight

If feels so right now, hold me tight,
Tell me I'm the only one,
And then I might,
Never be the lonely one.
So hold me tight, to-night, to-night,
It's you,
You you you – oo-oo – oo-oo.
Hold me tight,
Let me go on loving you,
To-night to-night,
Making love to only you,
So hold me tight, to-night, to-night,
It's you,
You you you – oo-oo – oo-oo.
Don't know what it means to hold you right,
Being here alone tonight with you,
If feels so right now, feels so right now.
Hold me tight,
Tell me I'm the only one,
And then I might,
Never be the only one,
So hold me tight, to-night, to-night,
It's you,
You you you – oo-oo – oo-oo.

Don't know what it means to hold you tight,
Being here alone tonight with you,
If feels so right now, feels so right now.
Hold me tight,
Let me go on loving you,
To-night to-night,
Making love to only you,
So hold me tight, to-night, to-night,
It's you,
You you you – oo-oo – oo-oo.

»Ich habe es wirklich satt, dass ich überall lese, ich wäre ein armer Einsiedler, der schrecklich unglücklich ist. Mir geht es großartig! Ich kann mir das alles nur so erklären, dass die Leute immer noch von mir erwarten, dass ich als Pressesprecher der Beatles auftrete, aber ich möchte mich einfach in Ruhe meiner Familie widmen.«
Paul

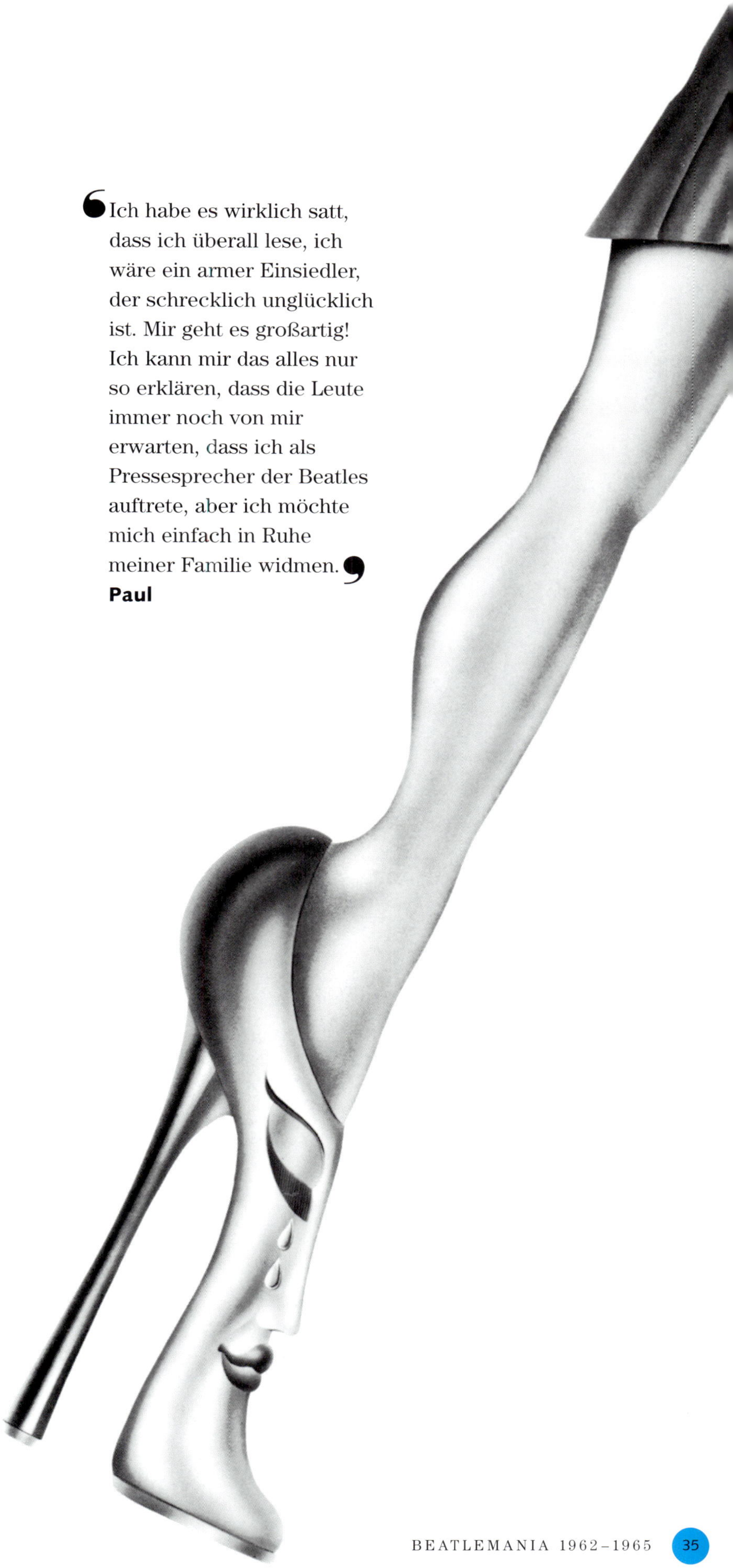

Ralph STEADman
20TH
CENTURY
FOR
20TH
CENTURY
DO
WOMEN'S
LIBERATION
FRONT
WOMEN'S
LIBERATION
FRONT

KISS ME!

I wanna be your man

I wanna be your lover baby,
I wanna be your lover baby,
I wanna be your man,
I wanna be your lover baby,
I wanna be your man.
Tell me that you love me baby,
like no other can,
love me like no other baby,
like no other can.
I wanna be your man,
I wanna be your man.
Tell me that you love me baby,
tell me you understand,
tell me that you love me baby,
I wanna be your man.
I wanna be your lover baby,
I wanna be your man.
I wanna be your lover baby,
I wanna be your man.
I wanna be your man.
I wanna be your man.
I wanna be your lover baby,
I wanna be your man.
Tell me that you love me baby,
like no other can,
love me like no other baby,
like no other can.
I wanna be your man,
I wanna be your man.

Not a second time

You know you made me cry,
I see no use in wond'ring why,
I cried for you.
And now, you've changed your mind,
I see no reason to change mine,
I cried, it's through, oh.
Oh, you're giving me the same old line,
I'm wond'ring why,
you hurt me then, you're back again,
no, no, not a second time.
You know you made me cry,
I see no use in wond'ring why,
I cried for you, yeh.
And now, you've changed your mind,
I see no reason to change mine,
I cried, it's through, oh.
Oh, you're giving me the same old line,
I'm wond'ring why,
you hurt me then, you're back again,
no, no, not a second time.

I want to hold your hand

Oh yeh, I'll tell you something,
I think you'll understand,
then I'll say that something,
I wanna hold your hand,
I wanna hold your hand,
I wanna hold your hand.
Oh please say to me
you'll let me be your man,
and please say to me
you'll let me hold your hand,
I wanna hold your hand.
And when I touch you
I feel happy inside,
it's such a feeling
that my love I can't hide,
I can't hide, I can't hide.
Yeh, you got that something,
I think you'll understand,
when I feel that something,
I wanna hold your hand,
I wanna hold your hand,
I wanna hold your hand.
And when I touch you
I feel happy inside,
it's such a feeling
that my love I can't hide,
I can't hide, I can't hide.
Yeh, you got that something,
I think you'll understand,
When I feel that something,
I wanna hold your hand,
I wanna hold your hand,
I wanna hold your hand.

„Die Übergänge von Tonika auf Submediante, von C-Dur nach a-Moll, und – in geringerem Ausmaß – der Mediantensprung (so bei I Want to Hold Your Hand) sind ein Charakteristikum der Lieder von Lennon/McCartney."
Der Musikkritiker der TIMES

This boy

That boy took my love away,
he'll regret it someday – i – ay,
but this boy wants you back again.
That boy isn't good for you,
tho' he may want you too,
this boy wants you back again.
Oh, and this boy would be happy,
just to love you, but oh my – yi – yi,
that boy won't be happy,
till he's seen you cry – hi – hi.
This boy wouldn't mind the pain,
would always feel the same,
if this boy gets you back again.
This boy. This boy.

❛...im Ausdruck ungewöhnlich, wegen der tragischen Musik, aber die Harmonien mit ihren Ketten von pan-diatonischen Clustern sind außerordentlich interessant...❜

William Mann, Musikkritiker der TIMES

WINDOLENE

I'll keep you satisfied

You don't need anybody to hold you,
here I stand with my arms open wide,
give me love and remember, what I told you,
I'll keep you satisfied.
You don't need anybody to kiss you,
ev'ry day I'll be here by your side,
don't go 'way, I'm afraid that I might miss you,
I'll keep you satisfied.
You can always get a simple thing like love anytime,
but it's diff'rent with a boy like me and a love like mine.
So believe ev'rything that I told you,
and agree that with me by your side,
you don't need anybody to hold you,
I'll keep you satisfied.
You can always get a simple thing like love anytime,
but it's diff'rent with a boy like me and a love like mine.
So believe ev'rything that I told you,
and agree that with me by your side,
you don't need anybody to hold you,
I'll keep you satisfied.
Give me love and remember, what I told you,
I'll keep you satisfied.

Released by Billy J Kramer and the Dakotas, November 1963

I'm in love

I've got something to tell you, I'm in love,
I've been longing to tell you, I'm in love.
You'll believe me, when I tell you, I'm in love with you.
You're my kind of girl,
You make me feel proud,
You make me want to shout aloud,
yes, I'm telling all my friends, I'm in love.
Ev'ry night I can't sleep, thinking of you,
and ev'ry little thing that you do,
yes, I'm telling all my friends, I'm in love.
Oh yeh, I'm sittin' on top of the world,
I'm in love with a wonderful girl,
and I never felt so good before,
if this is love, give me more, more, more.
Ev'ry night I can't sleep, thinking of you,
and ev'ry little thing that you do,
yes, I'm telling all my friends, I'm in love.
Yes, I'm telling all my friends, I'm in love,
in love.
Yes, I'm telling all my friends, I'm in love.

Released by Fourmost, February 1964

World without love

Please lock me away,
and don't allow the day
here inside, where I hide with my loneliness,
I don't care what they say,
I won't stay in a world without love.
Birds sing out of tune,
and rain clouds hide the moon,
I'm OK, here I'll stay with my loneliness,
I don't care what they say,
I won't stay in a world without love.
So I wait, and in a while
I will see my true love smile,
she may come, I know not when,
when she does I'll know,
so baby, until then –
Lock me away,
and don't allow the day
here inside where I hide with my loneliness,
I don't care what they say,
I won't stay in a world without love.
So I wait, and in a while
I will see my true love smile,
she may come, I know not when,
when she does I'll know,
so baby, until then –
Lock me away,
and don't allow the day
here inside where I hide with my loneliness,
I don't care what they say,
I won't stay in a world without love.
I don't care what they say,
I won't stay in a world without love.

Released by Peter and Gordon, March 1964

„Das I'm in Love habe ich für die Fourmost geschrieben."
John

„In jedem von uns steckt ein Hitler, aber in jedem von uns sind auch Liebe und Frieden. Geben wir doch endlich dem Frieden mal eine Chance!“
John

Coca-Cola

One and one is two

One and one is two,
what am I to do,
now that I'm in love with you.
I'm hoping ev'ry day
I'm gonna hear you say,
you really make my dreams come true.
Can't you feel, when I'm holding you near,
all the things I do.
show my love and I'm making it clear,
one and one is two.
One and one is two,
what am I to do,
now that I'm in love with you.
I'm hoping ev'ry day
I'm gonna hear you say,
you really make my dreams come true.
Can't you see, I loved you from the start,
don't you love me too?
I love you, but you're breaking my heart
from wanting you.
One and one is two,
what am I to do,
now that I'm in love with you
I'm hoping ev'ry day
I'm gonna hear you say,
you really make my dreams come true.
If you say that you're gonna be mine,
ev'rything's alright.
All the world would look so fine,
if you'd be mine tonight.
One and one is two.
What am I to do,
now that I'm in love with you.
I'm hoping ev'ry day
I'm gonna hear you say,
you really make my dreams come true.

Released by The Strangers, May 1964

❛Ich verstehe überhaupt nicht, wieso John sich beschwert, er hätte kein Geld. Wir brauchen doch gar keins. Wenn wir etwas wollen, unterschreiben wir einen Zettel und sagen, sie sollen die Rechnung an Apple schicken. Er hat doch seinen Wagen und das Haus, er hat doch alles, was er nur will.❜

Ringo

Nobody I know

Nobody I know could love me more than you,
You can give me so much love it seems untrue,
Listen to the bird who sings it to the tree,
And then when you've heard him see if you agree,
Nobody I know could love you more than me.
Ev'rywhere I go the sun comes shining through,
Ev'ryone I know is sure it shines for you,
Even in my dreams I look into your eyes,
Suddenly it seems I've found a paradise,
Ev'rywhere I go the sun comes shining through,
It means so much to be part of a heart of
a wonderful one,
When other lovers are gone we'll live on,
We'll live on.
Even in my dreams I look into your eyes,
Suddenly it seems I've found a paradise,
Ev'rywhere I go the sun comes shining through,
Nobody I know could love me more than you,
You can give me such love it seems untrue,
Listen to the bird who sings it to the tree,
And then when you've heard him see if you agree,
Nobody I know could love you more than me.
Nobody I know could love you more than me.

Released by Peter and Gordon, June 1964

I call your name

I call your name, but you're not there.
Was I to blame for being unfair?
Oh, I can't sleep at night since you've been gone,
I never weep at night, I can't go on.
Well, don't you know I can't take it?
I don't know who can.
I'm not goin' to make it,
I'm not that kind of man.
Oh, I can't sleep at night, but just the same,
I never weep at night, I call your name.
Well, don't you know I can't take it?
I don't know who can.
I'm not goin' to make it,
I'm not that kind of man.
Oh, I can't sleep at night, but just the same,
I never weep at night, I call your name.
I call your name.

Like dreamers do

Dreams, I saw a girl in my dreams.
And so it seems
that I will love her.
You, you are that girl in my dreams.
And so it seems
that I will love her.
And I yi, yi, waited for your kiss,
waited for the bliss.
Like dreamers do.
You, you came just one dream ago.
And now I know
that I will love you.
I knew, when you first said hello.
That's how I know
that I will love you.
And I yi, yi,
oh, I'll be there, yeh,
waiting for you, you.

Released by The Applejacks, July 1964

A hard day's night

It's been a hard day's night,
And I've been working like a dog,
It's been a hard day's night,
I should be sleeping like a log,
But when I get home to you,
I find the thing that you do,
Will make me feel alright.
You know I work all day,
To get you money to buy you things,
And it's worth it just to hear you say,
You're gonna give me ev'rything,
So why on earth should I moan,
'Cos when I get you alone,
You know I feel okay.
When I'm home ev'rything seems to be right
When I'm home feeling you holding me
tight, tight, yeh.
It's been a hard day's night,
And I've been working like a dog,
It's been a hard day's night,
I should be sleeping like a log,
But when I get home to you,
I find the thing that you do,
Will make me feel alright.
So why on earth should I moan,
'Cos when I get you alone,
You know I feel okay.
When I'm home ev'rything seems to be right,
When I'm home feeling you holding me
tight, tight, yeh.
It's been a hard day's night,
And I've been working like a dog,
It's been a hard day's night,
I should be sleeping like a log,
But when I get home to you,
I find the thing that you do,
Will make me feel alright.

❛Nicht Brian Epstein hat die Beatles entdeckt, sondern die Beatles haben Brian Epstein entdeckt.❜
Paul

I should have known better

I should have known better with a girl like you,
that I would love everything that you do,
and I do, hey hey, and I do.
Whoa, whoa, I never realised what a kiss could be,
this could only happen to me,
can't you see, can't you see?
That when I tell you that I love you, oh,
you're gonna say you love me too hoo hoo
hoo hoo, oh,
and when I ask you to be mine,
you're gonna say you love me too.
So, oh, I should have realised a lot of things before,
if this is love you've got to give me more,
give me more, hey hey, give me more.
Whoa, whoa, I never realised what a kiss could be,
this could only happen to me,
can't you see, can't you see?
That when I tell you that I love you, oh,
you're gonna say you love me too, oh
and when I ask you to be mine,
you're gonna say you love me too.
You love me too,
you love me too.

❛Ich spiele die Sitar jetzt nicht mehr. Um es richtig zu lernen, hätte ich bestimmt zehn Jahre gebraucht, und es gibt so viel anderes zu tun. Je besser ich sie kennen gelernt habe, desto klarer wurde mir, wie wenig ich wusste.❜

George

If I fell

If I fell in love with you would you promise to be true,
And help me understand?
'cos I've been in love before, and I found that love
was more,
Than just holding hands.
If I give my heart to you,
I must be sure from the very start,
That you would love me more than her.
If I trust in you, oh please,
Don't run and hide,
If I love you too, oh please don't hurt my pride like her.
'cos I couldn't stand the pain,
And I would be sad if our new love was in vain.
So I hope you see,
That I would love to love you,
And that she will cry when she learns we are two.
'cos I couldn't stand the pain,
And I would be sad if our new love was in vain.
So I hope you see,
That I would love to see you,
And that she will cry when she learns that we are two.
If I fell in love with you.

I'm happy just to dance with you

Before this dance is through,
I think I'll love you too,
I'm so happy when you dance with me.
I don't wanna kiss or hold your hand,
if it's funny, try an' understand.
There is really nothing else I'd rather do,
'cos I'm happy, just to dance with you.
I don't need to hug or hold you right,
I just wanna dance with you all night,
in this world there's nothing I would rather do,
'cos I'm happy just to dance with you.
Just to dance with you is everything I need,
before this dance is through,
I think I'll love you too,
I'm so happy when you dance with me.
if somebody tries to take my place,
let's pretend, we just can't see his face.
In this world there's nothing I would rather do,
'cos I'm happy just to dance with you.
Just to dance with you is everything I need,
before this dance is through,
I think I'll love you too,
I'm so happy when you dance with me.
If somebody tries to take my place,
let's pretend, we just can't see his face.
In this world there's nothing I would rather do,
I've discovered, I'm in love with you.
Oh, oh 'cos I'm happy just to dance with you.
Oh, oh.

»Ich habe dieses Lied für George geschrieben. Heute kann man überall lesen, Paul und ich hätten ihn nicht zur Geltung kommen lassen, aber das ist einfach nicht wahr. Ich habe ihn sehr unterstützt und ermutigt.«
John

And I love her

I give her all my love,
that's all I do,
and if you saw my love,
you'd love her too.
I love her.
She gives me ev'rything,
and tenderly,
the kiss my lover brings,
she brings to me,
and I love her.
A love like ours,
could never die,
as long as I,
have you near me.
Bright are the stars that shine,
dark is the sky,
I know this love of mine,
will never die,
and I love her.
Bright are the stars that shine,
dark is the sky,
I know this love of mine,
will never die,
and I love her.

Tell me why

Tell me why you cried,
and why you lied to me,
tell me why you cried,
and why you lied to me.
Well I gave you ev'rything I had,
but you left me sitting on my own,
did you have to treat me oh so bad,
all I do is hang my head and moan.
Tell me why you cried,
and why you lied to me,
tell me why your cried,
and why you lied to me.
If there's something I have said or done,
tell me what and I'll apologise,
if you don't I really can't go on,
holding back these tears in my eyes,
Tell me why you cried,
and why you lied to me,
tell me why you cried,
and why you lied to me.
Well I beg you on my bended knees,
if you'll only listen to my pleas,
is there anything I can do,
'cos I really can't stand it,
I'm so in love with you.
Tell me why you cried,
and why you lied to me.

for I don't care too much for money
for money can't buy me love

❛Ach, jeder soll alles und jedes so interpretieren, wie er mag. Mir ist das egal. Aber wenn da einer ankommt und sagt, Can't Buy Me Love besinge eine Nutte, dann reicht's mir. Das geht zu weit.❜
Paul

Can't buy me love

Can't buy me love, love,
Can't buy me love.
I'll buy you a diamond ring my friend,
If it makes you feel alright,
I'll get you anything my friend,
If it makes you feel alright,
For I don't care too much for money,
For money can't buy me love.
I'll give you all I've got to give,
If you say you love me too,
I may not have a lot to give,
But what I've got I'll give to you,
For I don't care too much for money.
For money can't buy me love.
Can't buy me love, ev'rybody tells me so,
Can't buy me love, no, no, no, no.
Say you don't want no diamond ring,
And I'll be satisfied,
Tell me that you want those kind of things,
That money just can't buy,
For I don't care too much for money,
For money can't buy me love.
Can't buy me love, ev'rybody tells me so,
Can't buy me love, no, no, no, no.
Say you don't want no diamond ring,
And I'll be satisfied,
Tell me that you want those kind of things,
That money just can't buy,
For I don't care too much for money,
For money can't buy me love.
Can't buy me love, ev'rybody tells me so,
Can't buy me love, no, no, no, no.
Can't buy me love, love,
Can't buy me love.

Anytime at all

Anytime at all,
anytime at all,
anytime at all,
all you've gotta do is call,
and I'll be there.
If you need somebody to love,
just look into my eyes,
I'll be there to make you feel right,
if you're feeling sorry and sad, I'd really sympathise.
Don't be sad, just call me tonight.
Anytime at all,
anytime at all,
anytime at all,
all you've gotta do is call,
and I'll be there.
If the sun has faded away,
I'll try to make it shine.
There is nothing I won't do,
If you need a shoulder to cry on, I hope it will be mine,
call me tonight and I'll come tonight.
Anytime at all,
anytime at all,
anytime at all,
all you've gotta do is call,
and I'll be there.
Anytime at all,
anytime at all,
anytime at all,
all you've gotta do is call,
And I'll be there.
Anytime at all,
all you've gotta do is call,
and I'll be there.

❛Das stammt auch aus der Zeit, als wir A Hard Day's Night gedreht haben. Ich schreibe heute nicht mehr so, aber ich glaube, dass ich es könnte, wenn ich wollte.❜
John

I'll cry instead

I've got every reason on earth to be mad,
'cos I've lost the only girl I had.
If I could get my way, I'd get myself
locked up today,
but I can't, so I'll cry instead.
I've got a chip on my shoulder that's
bigger than my feet.
I can't talk to people that I meet.
If I could see you now, I'd try to make you
say it somehow,
but I can't, so I'll cry instead.
Don't want to cry when there's people there,
I get shy when I start to stare.
I'm gonna hide myself away-ay-hay,
but I'll come back again some day.
And when I do you'd better hide all the girls,
I'm gonna break their hearts all round the world,
yes, I'm gonna break them in two and
show you what your lovin' man can do,
until then I'll cry instead.
Don't want to cry when there's people there,
I get shy when I start to stare.
I'm gonna hide myself away-ay-hay,
but I'll come back again some day.
And when I do you'd better hide all the girls,
I'm gonna break them in two and
show you what your lovin' man can do,
until then I'll cry instead.

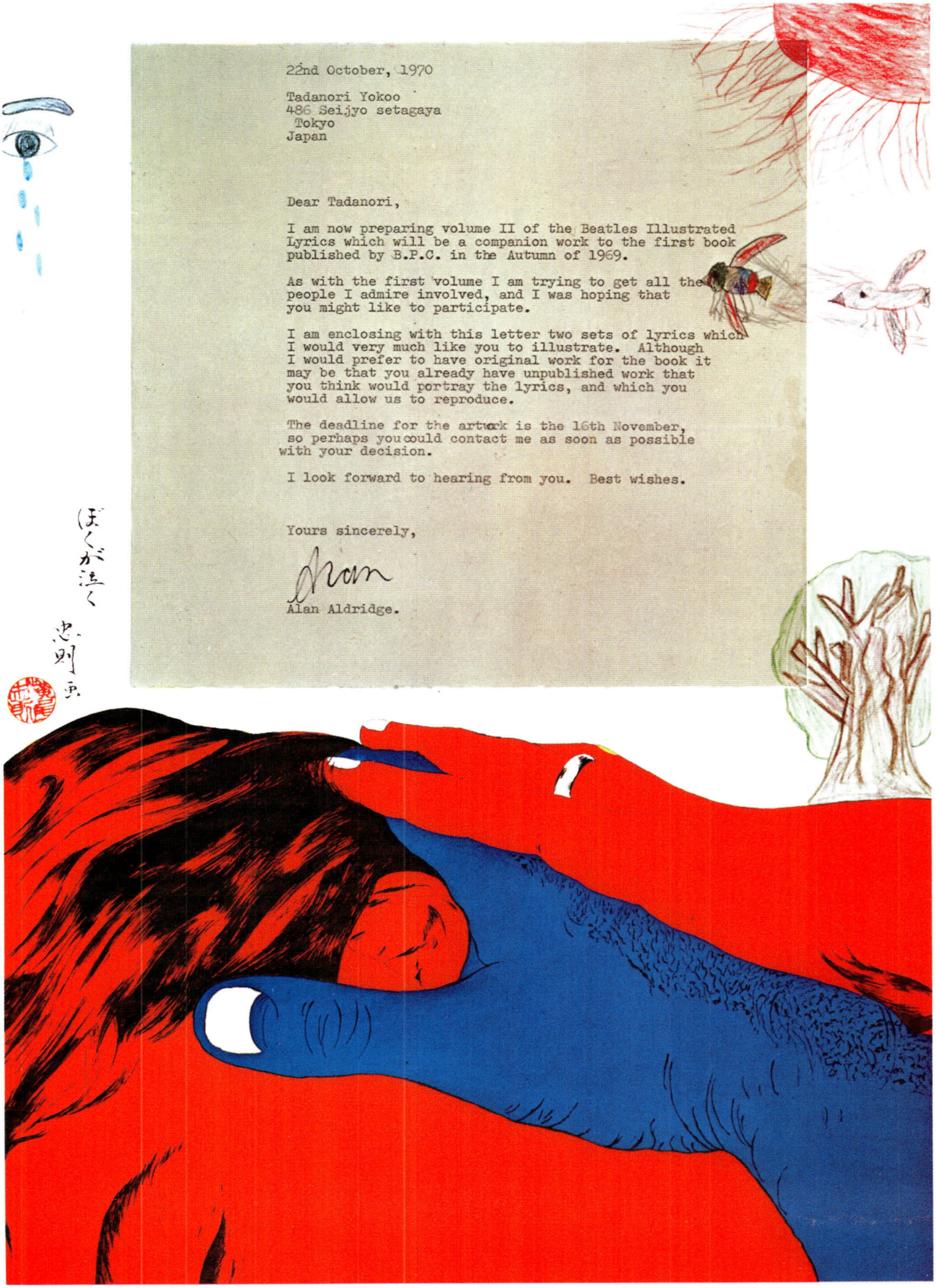

22nd October, 1970

Tadanori Yokoo
486 Seijyo setagaya
Tokyo
Japan

Dear Tadanori,

I am now preparing volume II of the Beatles Illustrated Lyrics which will be a companion work to the first book published by B.P.C. in the Autumn of 1969.

As with the first volume I am trying to get all the people I admire involved, and I was hoping that you might like to participate.

I am enclosing with this letter two sets of lyrics which I would very much like you to illustrate. Although I would prefer to have original work for the book it may be that you already have unpublished work that you think would portray the lyrics, and which you would allow us to reproduce.

The deadline for the artwork is the 16th November, so perhaps you could contact me as soon as possible with your decision.

I look forward to hearing from you. Best wishes.

Yours sincerely,

Alan

Alan Aldridge.

Things we said today

You say you will love me if I have to go,
you'll be thinking of me, somehow I will know,
someday when I'm lonely, wishing you weren't so
far away,
then I will remember things we said today.
You say you will be mine, girl, till the end of time,
these days such a kind girl seems so hard to find,
someday when we're dreaming, deep in love,
not a lot to say,
then I will remember things we said today.
Me I'm just a lucky kind,
love to hear you say that love is love,
and though we may be blind,
love is here to stay.
And that's enough to make you mine girl,
be the only one,
love me all the time girl, we'll go on and on,
someday when we're dreaming, deep in love,
not a lot to say,
then we will remember things we said today.
Me I'm just a lucky kind,
love to hear you say that love is love
and though we may be blind,
love is here to stay.
And that's enough to make you mine girl,
be the only one,
love me all the time girl, we'll go on and on,
someday when we're dreaming, deep in love,
not a lot to say,
then we will remember things we said today.

»Am schönsten ist es immer noch,
wenn man die Zeitungen aufschlägt
und seinen Namen nicht darin findet.«
George

When I get home

Whoa-ho, whoa-ho,
I got a whole lot of things to tell her, when
I get home.
Come on, I'm on my way,
'cos I'm gonna see my baby today,
I've got a whole lot of things I've gotta say to her.
Whoa-ho, whoa-ho,
I got a whole lot of things to tell her, when
I get home.
Come on if you please,
I've got no time for trivialities,
I've got a girl who's waiting home for me tonight.
Whoa-ho, whoa-ho,
I got a whole lot of things to tell her, when
I get home.
When I'm getting home tonight, I'm gonna hold her tight,
I'm gonna love her more,
till I walk out that door – again.
Come on, let me through,
I've got so many things to, I've got to do,
I've got not business being here with you this way.
Whoa-ho, whoa-ho,
I got a whole lot of things to tell her, when
I get home – Yeah.

»Das ist für mich immer noch
das Größte: wenn ich mich in
Liverpool in den Bus setzen
kann und nach Cheshire aufs
Land fahre.«
Paul

家に帰れば
TELEGRAM
NIPPON TELEGRAPH & TELEPHONE PUBLIC CORPORATION
3004 0683 046C B KXB1401 LAJ940
RFZ620X TLB680 JPTK CO
GBLB 022 LONDONLB TF 22
成城町486
ヨコオタダノリ様
18 1118
SETAGAYA TOK 18.11.70 JAPAN
TADANORI YOKOO 486 SEIJYO SETAGAYA TOKYO
PLEASE ILLUSTRATE BOTH BEATLES SONGS STOP
ART WORK TO REACH ME BY 10TH DECEMBER
ALAN ALDRIDGE
13
13
NOV 18 PM.8.57
忠則

You can't do that

I got something to say that might cause you pain,
if I catch you talking to that boy again,
I'm gonna let you down,
and leave you flat,
because I told you before, oh,
you can't do that.
Well, it's the second time, I've caught you talking to him,
do I have to tell you one more time, I think it's a sin,
I think I'll let you down.
Let you down and leave you flat,
gonna let you down and leave you flat,
because I've told you before, oh,
you can't do that.
Ev'rybody's green,
'cause I'm the one, who won your love,
but if it's seen,
you're talking that way
they'd laugh in my face.
So please listen to me, if you wanna stay mine,
I can't help my feelings, I'll go out of my mind,
I know I'll let you down,
and leave you flat,
gonna let you down and leave you flat,
because I've told you before, oh,
you can't do that.
Ev'rybody's green,
'cause I'm the one, who won your love,
but if it's seen,
you're talking that way
they'd laugh in my face.
So please listen to me, if you wanna stay mine,
I can't help my feelings, I'll go out of my mind,
I know I'll let you down,
and leave you flat,
gonna let you down and leave you flat,
because I've told you before, oh,
you can't do that.

„Das war damals mein Versuch, Wilson Pickett zu sein, aber das Lied ist nur die B-Seite geworden, denn Can't Buy Me Love war so gut."
John

I'll be back

You know if you break my heart, I'll go but I'll be back again,
'cos I told you once before good-bye, but I came back again,
I love you so – oh, I'm the one who wants you oh, oh.
You could find better things to do, than to break my heart again,
this time I will show that I'm not trying to pretend,
I thought that you would realise,
that if I ran away from you,
that you would want me too,
but I've got a big surprise oh, oh.
Oh, you could find better things to do than to break my heart again,
this time I will try to show that I'm not trying to pretend,
I wanna go, but I hate to leave you,
you know, I hate to leave you oh, oh.
Oh, you if you break my heart, I'll go,
but I'll be back again.

It's for you

I'd say some day,
I'm bound to give my heart away,
when I do, it's for you.
Love, true love,
seems to be all I'm thinking of,
but it's true, it's for you.
They said that love was a lie,
told me that I should never try to find
somebody who'd be kind, kind to only me.
So I just tell them, they're right, who wants a fight?
Tell them, I quite agree, nobody'd love me,
then I look at you, and
love comes, love shows,
I give my heart and no-one knows that I do,
it's for you,
it's for you.

Released by Cilla Black, August 1964

„Ich bin eifersüchtig auf den Spiegel."
John

Barbara Nessim

From a window

Late yesterday night, I saw a light shine from a window,
and as I looked again, your face came into sight.
I couldn't walk on until you'd gone from your window.
I had to make you mine, I knew you were the one.
Oh, I would be so glad just to have a love like that,
oh, I would be true and I'd live my life for you.
So meet me tonight, just where the light shines from a window,
and as I take your hand, say that you'll be mine tonight.
Oh, I would be so glad just to have a love like that,
oh, I would be so true and I'd live my life for you.
So meet me tonight, just where the light shines from a window,
and as I take your hand, say that you'll be mine tonight.

Released by Billy J Kramer and the Dakotas, August 1964

I don't want to see you again

I don't want to see you again.
I hear that love is planned,
how can I understand,
when someone says to me,
'I don't want to see you again.'?
Why do I cry at night?
Something wrong could be right.
I hear you say to me,
'I don't want to see you again.'
As you turned your back on me,
you hid the light of day.
I didn't have to play,
at being broken hearted.
I know that later on,
after love's been and gone,
I'd still hear someone say,
'I don't want to see you again.'
As you turned your back on me,
you hid the light of day.
I didn't have to play,
at being broken hearted.
I hear that love is planned,
how can I understand,
when someone says to me,
'I don't want to see you again.'?
I don't want to see you again.

Released by Peter and Gordon, September 1964

I feel fine

Baby's good to me, you know,
she's happy as can be, you know,
she said so.
I'm in love with her and I feel fine.
Baby says she's mine you know,
she tells me all the time you know,
she said so.
I'm in love with her and I feel fine.
I'm so glad that she's my little girl,
she's so glad she's telling all the world.
That her baby buys her things you know,
he buys her diamond rings you know,
she said so.
She's in love with me and I feel fine.
Baby says she's mine you know,
she tells me all the time you know,
she said so.
I'm in love with her and I feel fine.
I'm so glad that she's my little girl,
she's so glad she's telling all the world.
That her baby buys her things you know,
he buys her diamond rings you know,
she said so.
She's in love with me and I feel fine.

❛Das habe ich bei einer Aufnahmesitzung geschrieben. Es ist alles am Gitarren-Riff aufgehängt, mit dem es beginnt.❜
John

She's a woman

My love don't give me presents.
I know that she's no peasant,
only ever has to give me love forever and forever,
my love don't give me presents,
turn me on when I get lonely,
people tell me that she's only foolin',
I know she isn't.
She don't give the boys the eye,
she hates to see me cry,
she is happy just to hear me say that I
will never leave her.
She don't give the boys the eye,
she will never make me jealous,
gives me all her time as well as lovin',
don't ask me why.
She's a woman who understands.
She's a woman who loves her man.
My love don't give me presents.
I know that she's no peasant,
only ever has to give me love forever and forever,
my love don't give me presents,
turn me on when I get lonely,
people tell me that she's only foolin',
I know she isn't.
She's a woman who understands.
She's a woman who loves her man.
My love don't give me presents.
I know that she's no peasant,
only ever has to give me love forever and forever,
my love don't give me presents,
turn me on when I get lonely,
people tell me that she's only foolin',
I know she isn't.
She's a woman, she's a woman.

Eight days a week

Ooh I need your love babe, guess you know it's true,
hope you need my love babe just like I need you,
hold me, love me,
hold me, love me,
ain't got nothin' but love babe,
eight days a week.
Love you ev'ry day girl, always on my mind,
one thing I can say girl, love you all the time,
hold me, love me,
hold me, love me,
ain't got nothin' but love babe,
eight days a week.
Eight days a week I love you,
eight days a week is not enough to show I care.
Ooh I need your love babe, guess you know it's true,
hope you need my love babe just like I need you,
hold me, love me,
hold me, love me,
ain't got nothin' but love babe,
eight days a week.
Eight days a week I love you,
eight days a week is not enough to show I care.
Love you ev'ry day girl, always on my mind,
one thing I can say girl, love you all the time,
hold me, love me,
hold me, love me,
ain't got nothin' but love babe,
eight days a week.
Eight days a week. Eight days a week.

❛Eigentlich wollen wir bloß
vier Rock'n'Roller sein,
aber das dürfen wir nicht.
Wegen Apple. Wir müssen
Geschäftsleute werden.❜
Ringo

I'm a loser

I'm a loser, I'm a loser,
And I'm not what I appear to be.
Of all the love I have won or have lost,
There is one love I should never have crossed.
She was a girl in a million my friend,
I should have known she would win in the end.
I'm a loser, and I lost someone who's near to me,
I'm a loser, and I'm not what I appear to be.
Although I laugh and I act like a clown,
Beneath this mask, I am wearing a frown,
My tears are falling like rain from the sky,
Is it for her or myself that I cry.
I'm a loser, and I lost someone who's near to me,
I'm a loser, and I'm not what I appear to be.
What have I done to deserve such a fate,
I realise I have left it far too late.
And so it's true pride comes before a fall,
I'm telling you so that you won't lose all.
I'm a loser, and I lost someone who's near to me,
I'm a loser, and I'm not what I appear to be.

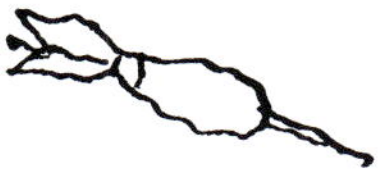

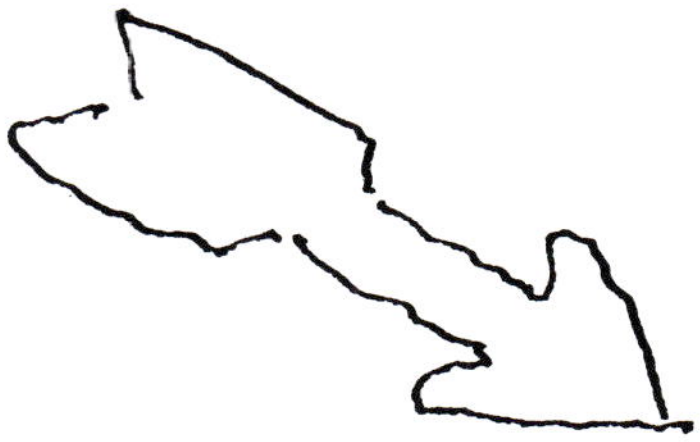

No reply

This happened once before,
when I came to your door, no reply.
They said it wasn't you,
but I saw you peep through your window,
I saw the light, I saw the light,
I know that you saw me,
'cos I looked up to see your face.
I tried to telephone,
they said you were not home, that's a lie,
'cos I know where you've been,
I saw you walk in your door,
I nearly died, I nearly died,
'cos you walked hand in hand
with another man in my place.
If I were you I'd realise that I
love you more that any other guy,
and I'll forgive the lies that I
heard before when you gave me no reply.
I've tried to telephone,
they said you were not home, that's a lie,
'cos I know where you've been,
I saw you walk in your door,
I nearly died, I nearly died,
'cos you walked hand in hand
with another man in my place.
No reply, no reply.

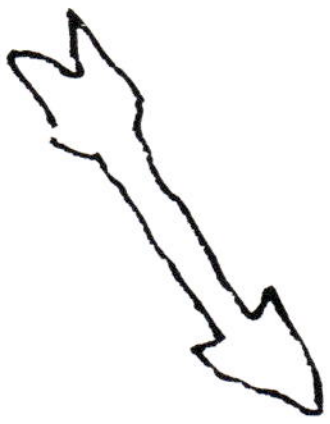

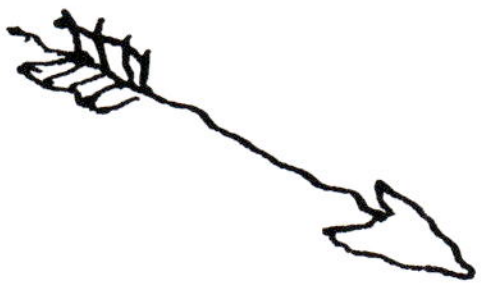

❛Die größten Komponisten
seit Ludwig van Beethoven.❜
Richard Buckle
in der SUNDAY TIMES,
Dezember 1963

I don't want to spoil the party

I don't want to spoil the party so I'll go,
I would hate my disappointment to show,
there's nothing for me here so I will disappear,
if she turns up while I'm gone please let me know.
I've had a drink or two and I don't care,
there's no fun in what I do if she's not there,
I wonder what went wrong I've waited far too long,
I think I'll talk a walk and look for her.
Though tonight she's made me sad,
I still love her.
If I find her I'll be glad,
I still love her.
I don't want to spoil the party so I'll go,
I would hate my disappointment to show,
there's nothing for me here so I will disappear,
if she turns up while I'm gone please let me know.
Though tonight she's made me sad,
I still love her.
If I find her I'll be glad,
I still love her.
I've had a drink or two and I don't care,
there's no fun in what I do if she's not there,
I wonder what went wrong I've waited far too long,
I think I'll take a walk and look for her.

„Eine ganz persönliche Sache.
In den ersten Jahren schrieb
ich weniger Lieder als Paul,
weil er besser Gitarre spielte.
Beim Gitarrespielen hat er mir
wirklich viel beigebracht."
John

I'll follow the sun

One day you'll look to see I've gone,
for tomorrow may rain so I'll follow the sun.
Some day you'll know I was the one,
but tomorrow may rain so I'll follow the sun.
And now the time has come and so my love I must go,
and though I lose a friend in the end you will know, oh
One day you'll look to see I've gone,
for tomorrow may rain so I'll follow the sun.
And now the time has come and so my love I must go,
and though I lose a friend in the end you will know, oh
One day you'll look to see I've gone,
for tomorrow may rain so I'll follow the sun.

❝Unser Leben auf der Farm hier in Schottland ist überhaupt erst das richtige Leben. Das Leben ist hart hier, aber es ist die Sorte Leben, von der ich immer geträumt habe. Ich liebe die Natur. Als ich ein Kind war, haben wir oft mit der Schule Wanderungen gemacht, ich fand es immer ganz toll, wenn uns der Lehrer die Vogelarten erklärte.❞
Paul

Baby's in black

Oh dear, what can I do?
Baby's in black and I'm feeling blue,
Tell me, oh what can I do?
She thinks of him and so she dresses in black,
And though he'll never come back, she's dressed in black.
Oh dear, what can I do?
Baby's in black and I'm feeling blue,
Tell me, oh what can I do?
I think of her, but she only thinks of him,
and though it's only a whim, she thinks of him.
Oh how long will it take,
Till she sees the mistake she has made?
Dear what can I do?
Baby's in black and I'm feeling blue,
Tell me, oh what can I do?
Oh how long will it take,
Till she sees the mistake she has made?
Dear what can I do?
Baby's in black and I'm feeling blue,
Tell me, oh what can I do?
She thinks of him and so she dresses in black,
And though he'll never come back, she's dressed in black.
Oh dear, what can I do?
Baby's in black and I'm feeling blue,
Tell me, oh what can I do?

Every little thing

When I'm walking behind her,
people tell me I'm lucky,
yes I know I'm a lucky guy,
I remember the first time
I was lonely without her,
yes, I'm thinking about her now.
Ev'ry little thing she does,
she does for me, hey,
and you know the things she does,
she does for me, oh.
When I'm with her I'm happy,
Just to know that she loves me now.
There is one thing I am sure of,
I will love her forever,
for I know love will never die.
Ev'ry little thing she does,
she does for me, yeh,
and you know the things she does,
she does for me, oh.
Ev'ry little thing she does,
she does for me, yeh,
and you know the things she does,
she does for me, oh.

What you're doing

Look what you're doing, I'm feeling blue and lonely,
would it be too much to ask of you,
what you're doing to me?
You got me running and there's no fun in it,
why should it be so much to ask of you,
what you're doing to me?
I've been waiting here for you,
wond'ring what you're gonna do,
should you need a love that's true, it's me.
Please stop your lying, you've got me crying, girl,
why should it be so much to ask of you,
what you're doing to me?
I've been waiting here for you,
wond'ring what you're gonna do,
should you need a love that's true, it's me.
Please stop your lying, you've got me crying, girl,
why should it be so much to ask of you,
what you're doing to me?
What you're doing to me.

Yes it is

If you wear red tonight,
remember what I said tonight,
for red is the colour my baby wore,
and what's more, it's true,
yes it is.
Scarlet were the clothes she wore,
ev'rybody knows I'm sure,
I would remember all the things we planned,
understand it's true,
yes, it is true,
yes it is.
I could be happy with you by my side,
if I could forget her,
but it's my pride,
yes it is, yes it is,
Please don't wear red tonight,
that is what I said tonight,
for red is the colour that will make me blue,
in spite of you, it's true,
yes it is, it's true,
yes it is.
I could be happy with you by my side,
if I could forget her,
but it's my pride,
yes it is, yes it is.
Please don't wear red tonight,
this is what I said tonight,
for red is the colour that will make me blue,
in spite of you it's true,
yes it is, it's true.

I'm down

You tell lies thinking I can't see,
You can't cry 'cos you're laughing at me,
I'm down (I'm really down),
I'm down (down on the ground),
I'm down (I'm really down).
How can you laugh,
when you know I'm down? (How can you laugh?).
Man buys ring woman throws it away,
same old thing happens ev'ry day,
I'm down (I'm really down),
I'm down (down on the ground),
I'm down (I'm really down).
How can you laugh,
when you know I'm down? (How can you laugh?).
We're all alone and there's nobody else,
you still moan 'Keep your hands to yourself',
I'm down (I'm really down),
I'm down (down to the ground),
I'm down (I'm really down).
How can you laugh,
when you know I'm down? (How can you laugh?).
Oh yeah.

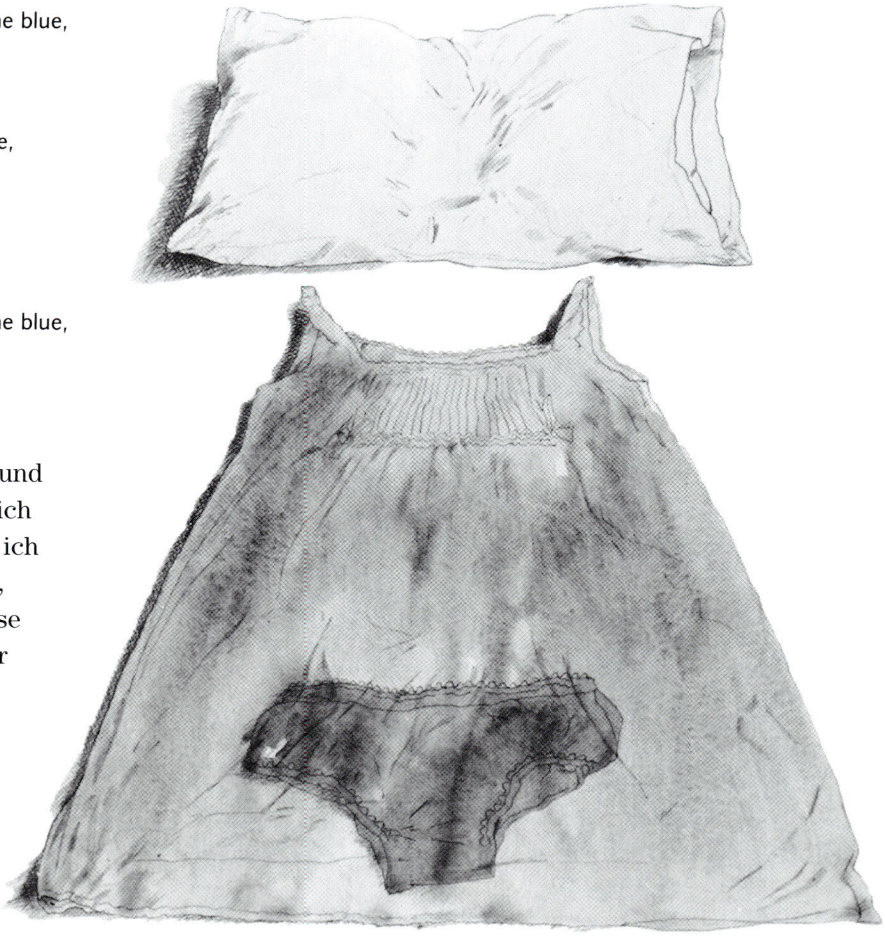

❛Wir sind bescheiden, natürlich und durch und durch britisch. Neulich bin ich gefragt worden, warum ich meine Ringe an der Hand trage, und ich habe gesagt, an der Nase hielten sie nicht. Das wollte mir der Bursche nicht glauben.❜
Ringo

Help

Help! I need somebody,
help! Not just anybody,
help! You know I need someone,
help!
When I was younger, so much younger than today,
I never needed anybody's help in any way,
but now those days are gone I'm not so self assured,
now I find I've changed my mind I've
opened up the doors.
Help me if you can, I'm feeling down,
and I do appreciate you being around,
help me get my feet back on the ground,
won't you please please help me?
And now my life has changed in oh so many ways,
my independence seems to vanish in the haze,
but ev'ry now and then I feel so insecure,
I know that I just need you like I've never done before.
Help me if you can, I'm feeling down,
and I do appreciate you being around,
help me get my feet back on the ground,
won't you please please help me?
When I was younger, so much younger than today,
I never needed anybody's help in any way,
but now those days are gone I'm not so self assured,
now I find I've changed my mind I've
opened up the doors.
Help me if you can, I'm feeling down,
and I do appreciate you being around,
help me get my feet back on the ground,
won't you please please help me?
Help me. Help me.

❛Help hat viel Spaß gemacht, aber es war nicht unser Film. Wir waren da nur so als Gäste vertreten. Ja, es war Spaß, aber als Filmidee war's im Grunde nicht ganz das Richtige für uns.❜
Paul

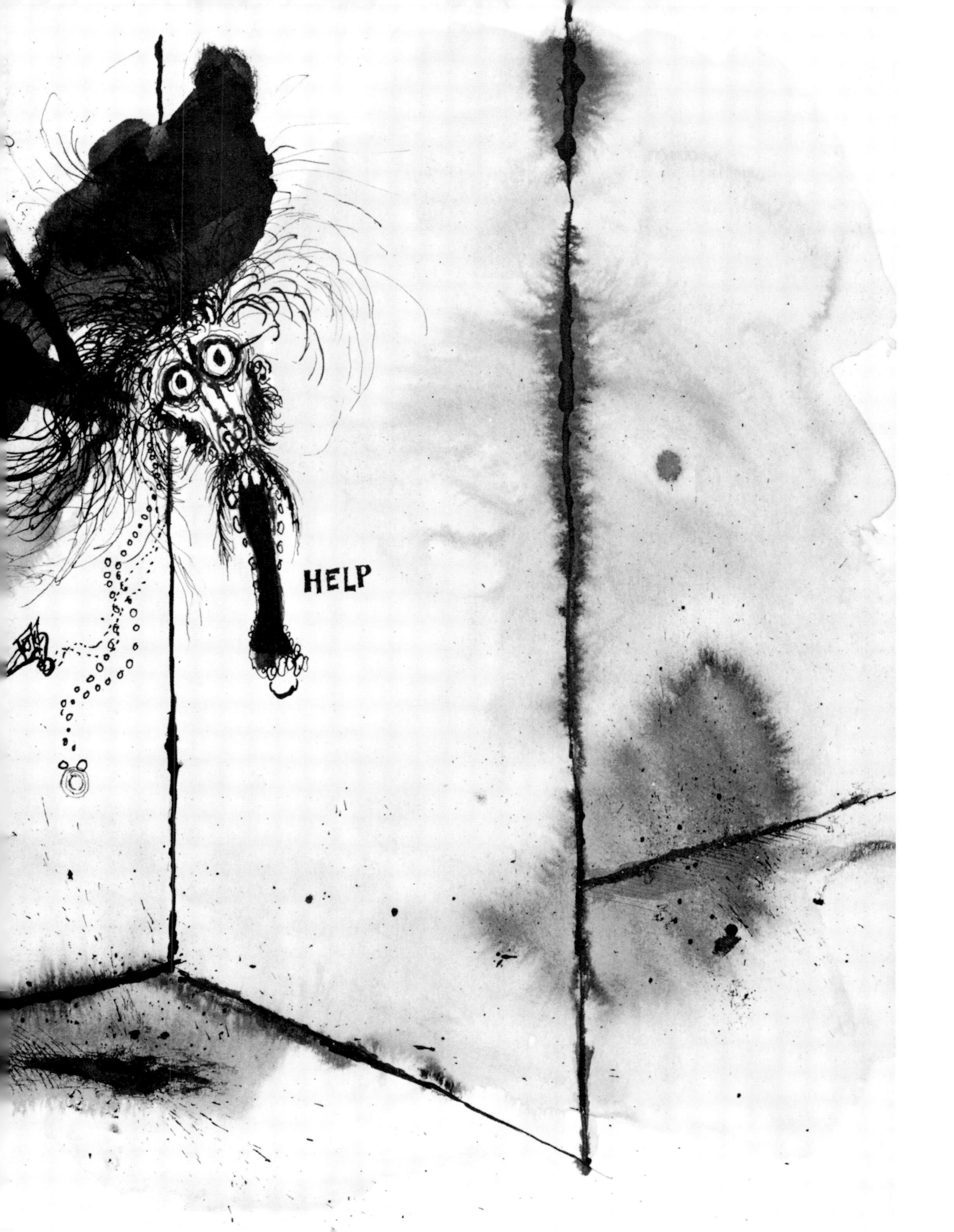
HELP

The night before

We said our goodbyes (on the night before),
love was in your eyes
now today I find, you have changed your mind,
treat me like you did the night before.
Were you telling lies (on the night before)?
Was I so unwise (on the night before)?
When I held you near, you were so sincere,
treat me like you did the night before.
Last night is the night I will remember you by,
when I think of things you did it makes me wanna cry.
We said our goodbyes (on the night before),
love was in your eyes
now today I find you have changed your mind,
treat me like you did the night before.
When I held you near, you were so sincere,
treat me like you did the night before.
Last night is the night I will remember you by,
when I think of things we did it makes me wanna cry.
Were you telling lies (on the night before)?
Was I so unwise?
When I held you near, you were so sincere,
treat me like you did the night before.

„Wie oft uns ein Auftritt wirklich Spaß gemacht hat? Vielleicht ein einziger auf einer wochenlangen Tournee. Dieses ganze Gerede über Clubs und Shows ist eine Illusion – ein Alptraum. Von dreißig Auftritten ist einer wirklich befriedigend, und um den zu erleben, muss man so viele schauderhafte Abende durchstehen."

John

You've got to hide your love away

Here I stand with head in hand,
turn my face to the wall.
If she's gone I can't go on,
feeling two foot small.
Ev'rywhere people stare,
each and ev'ry day.
I can see them laugh at me,
and I hear them say.
Hey, you've got to hide your love away.
Hey, you've got to hide your love away.
How can I even try,
I can never win,
hearing them, seeing them,
in the state I'm in.
How could she say to me
love will find a way?
Gather round all you clowns
let me hear you say.
Hey, you've got to hide your love away.
Hey, you've got to hide your love away.

Another girl

For I have got another girl, another girl,
you're making me say that I ve got nobody but you,
but as from today well I've got somebody that's new,
I ain't no fool and I don't take what I don't want,
for I have got another girl, another girl.
She's sweeter than all the girls and I've met quite
a few,
nobody in the world can do what she can do,
and so I'm telling you this time you'd better stop,
for I have got another girl.
Another girl, who will love me till the end,
through thick and thin she will always be my friend.
I don't wanna say that I've been unhappy with you,
but as from today well I've seen somebody that's
new,
I ain't no fool and I don't take what I don't want,
for I have got another girl.
Another girl, who will love me till the end,
through thick and think she will always be my friend.
I don't wanna say that I've been unhappy with you,
but as from today well I've seen somebody that's
new,
I ain't no fool and I don't take what I don't want,
for I have got another girl.

❛Ich liebe Yoko.
Ich liebe Cynthia nicht.❜
John
gegenüber Reportern, die ihn über das Ende seiner ersten Ehe ausfragen wollten

❛Das ist eins von meinen. Damals haben mich die Texte noch nicht interessiert. Ich dachte, die Worte wären egal. Bob Dylan sagte immer, ›Du musst auf die Worte achten, Mann‹, wenn er wieder eines seiner Produkte herausbrachte. Und ich habe gesagt, ich höre nicht auf die Worte.❜
John

You're going to lose that girl

You're going to lose that girl,
you're going to lose that girl.
If you don't take her out tonight, she's
going to change her mind,
and I will take her out tonight, and I will
treat her kind.
You're going to lose that girl,
you're going to lose that girl.
If you don't treat her right, my friend,
you're going to find her gone,
'cos I will treat her right, and then you'll
be the lonely one.
You're going to lose that girl,
you're going to lose that girl.
I'll make a point of taking her away from you, yeah,
the way you treat her what else can I do?
You're going to lose that girl,
you're going to lose that girl.
I'll make a point of taking her away from you, yeah,
the way you treat her what else can I do?
If you don't take her out tonight, she's
going to change her mind,
and I will take her out tonight, and I will
treat her kind.
You're going to lose that girl,
you're going to lose that girl.

Another Girl

Ticket to ride

I think I'm gonna be sad,
I think it's today yeh,
The girl that's driving me mad,
Is going away.
She's got a ticket to ride,
She's got a ticket to ri-hi-hide,
She's got a ticket to ride, but she don't care.
She said that living with me,
Is bringing her down yeh,
For she would never be free,
When I was around.
She's got a ticket to ride,
She's got a ticket to ri-hi-hide,
She's got a ticket to ride, but she don't care.
I don't know why she's riding so high,
She ought to think twice,
She ought to do right by me,
Before she gets to saying goodbye,
She ought to think twice,
She ought to do right by me.
I think I'm gonna be sad,
I think it's today yeh,
The girl that's driving me mad,
Is going away.
She's got a ticket to ride,
She's got a ticket to ri-hi-hide,
She's got a ticket to ride, but she don't care.
I don't know why she's riding so high,
She ought to think twice,
She ought to do right by me,
Before she gets to saying goodbye,
She ought to think twice,
She ought to do right by me.
She said that living with me,
Is bringing her down yeh,
For she would never be free,
When I was around.
She's got a ticket to ride,
She's got a ticket to ri-hi-hide,
She's got a ticket to ride, but she don't care.
My baby don't care, my baby don't care.

It's only love

I get high when I see you go by,
my oh my,
when you sigh, my, my inside just dries,
butterflies,
why am I so shy when I'm beside you?
It's only love and that is all,
why should I feel the way I do?
It's only love and that is all,
but it's so hard loving you.
Is it right that you and I should fight
every night?
Just the sight of you makes night time bright,
very bright.
Haven't I the right to make it up, girl?
It's only love and that is all,
why should I feel the way I do?
It's only love and that is all,
but it's so hard loving you.
Yes, it's so hard loving you, oh.

»Die Art und Weise, wie sie Yoko am Anfang behandelt haben, kann ich Paul und George nicht verzeihen, aber das ändert nichts daran, dass ich die beiden immer noch lieb habe.«
John

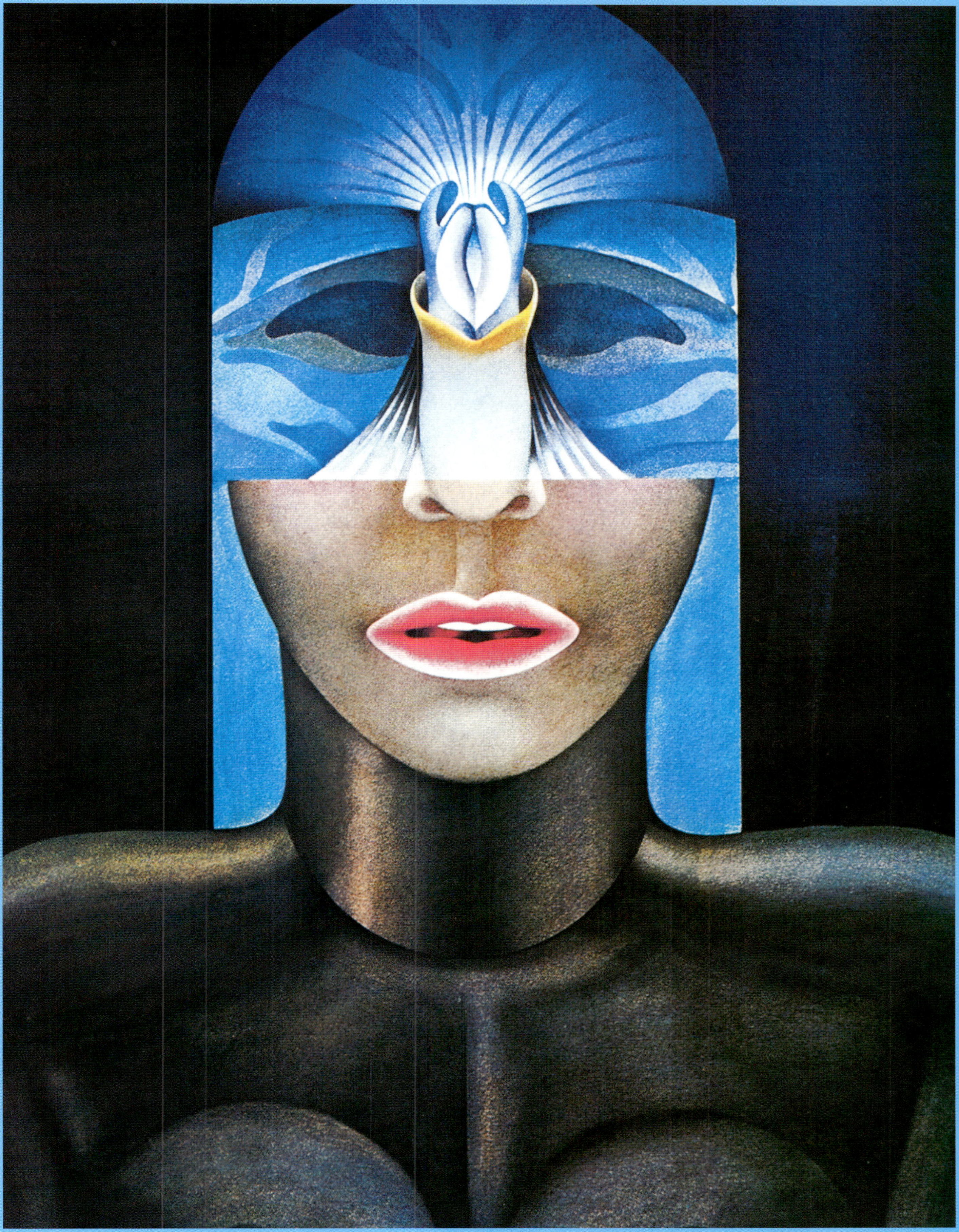

Tell me what you see

If you let me take your heart I will prove to you,
we will never be apart if I'm part of you,
open up your eyes now tell me what you see,
it is no surprise now what you see is me.
Big and black the clouds may be time will pass away,
if you put your trust in me I'll make bright your day.
Look into these eyes now, tell me what you see,
don't you realise now what you see is me.
Tell me what you see.
Listen to me one more time how can I get through,
can't you try to see that I'm trying to get to you,
open up your eyes now tell me what you see,
it is no surprise now, what you see is me.
Tell me what you see.
Listen to me one more time how can I get through,
Listen to me one more time how can I get through,
can't you try to see that I'm trying to get to you,
open up your eyes now tell me what you see,
it is no surprise what you see is me.

I've just seen a face

I've just seen a face I can't forget the time
or place where we met,
she's just the girl for me and I want the
world to see we've met.
mm mm
Had it been another day I might have
looked the other way and,
I'd have never been aware but as it is I'll
dream of her tonight.
da da
Falling, yes I'm falling,
and she keeps calling me back again.
I have never known the like of this I've
been alone and I have,
missed things and kept out of sight for
other girls were never quite like this.
da da
Falling, yes I'm falling,
and she keeps calling me back again.
mm mm
I've just seen a face I can't forget the time
or place where we met,
she's just the girl for me and I want the
world to see we've met.
mm mm
Falling, yes, I'm falling,
and she keeps calling me back again.

"Ich wäre gern reich und berühmt und gleichzeitig unsichtbar, damit wir den Ruhm und den Spaß hätten, aber uns niemand erkennt, wenn wir auf der Straße herumlaufen."
John

Yesterday

Yesterday, all my troubles seemed so far away,
Now it looks as though they're here to stay,
Oh I believe in yesterday.
Suddenly, I'm not half the man I used to be,
There's a shadow hanging over me,
Oh yesterday came suddenly …
Why she had to go I don't know. She wouldn't say.
I said something wrong, now I long for yesterday.
Yesterday, love was such an easy game to play,
Now I need a place to hide away,
Oh, I believe in yesterday …

›Einmal wachte ich vormittags auf und ging ans Klavier, und ich klimperte so dahin, und dieses Lied kam seines Weges. Das ist es, was passiert: Sie kommen einfach daher. Doch mir fiel kein Text dazu ein, und ich taufte es ›Spiegelei‹, und so hieß es auch zwei Vormittage lang. Dann kam ich auf ›Yesterday‹. Die Worte begannen zu plätschern, und wir hatten ein Lied.‹
Paul

II

The Sergeant's Mystery Tour
1965→1968

That means a lot

A friend says that your love won't mean a lot.
And you know that your love is all you got.
At times they go so fine
and at times they're not.
But when she says, she loves you,
that means a lot.
A friend says that a love is never true.
And you know that this could apply to you.
A church can mean so much,
when it's all you got.
But when she says, she loves you,
that means a lot.
Love can be deep inside,
love can be suicide.
Can't you see, you can't hide
what you feel when it's real.
When she says she loves you,
that means a lot.
Can't you see?

Released by P J Proby, September 1965

Day tripper

Got a good reason for taking the easy way out,
got a good reason for taking the easy way out – now,
she was a day tripper,
one way ticket, yeh,
it took me so long to find out, and I found out.
She's a big teaser, she took me half the way there,
she's a big teaser, she took me half the way there – now,
she was a day tripper,
one way ticket, yeh,
it took me so long to find out, and I found out.
Tried to please her, she only played one night stands,
tried to please her, she only played one night stands – now,
she was a day tripper,
Sunday driver, yeh,
it took me so long to find out, and I found out.
Day tripper, yeh.

"Drop me a line with all the news, I've got a little bit behind The Times down here!"

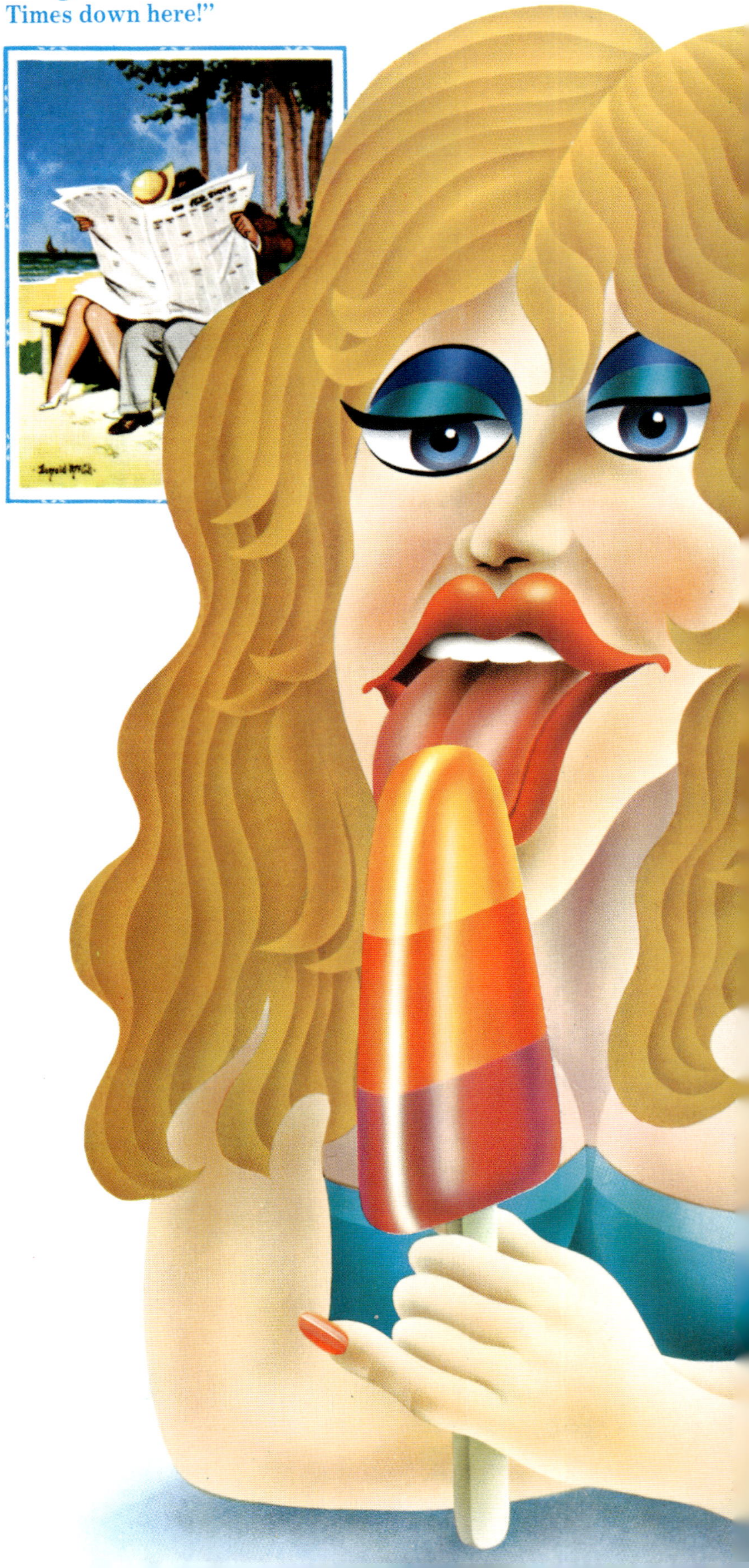

"I can't get my winkle out
Isn't it a sin?
The more I try to get it out
The further it goes in!"

"You'd never believe the liberties the men take down here. Perfect strangers too!"

"Oh, go on, Dick. The further your in the nicer it feels"

"I SUPPOSE YOU FIND THIS RATHER FLAT AFTER THE ALPS, MR. MOUNTWELL?"

"KIDS HIMSELF HE'S A GREAT LOVER—STARTS OFF WELL, BUT CAN'T KEEP IT UP!"

We can work it out

Try to see it my way,
do I have to keep on talking till I can't go on?
While you see it your way,
run the risk of knowing that our love may
soon be gone.
We can work it out. We can work it out.
Think of what you're saying,
you can get it wrong and still you think
that it's alright,
think of what I'm saying,
we can work it out and get it straight, or
say good-night.
We can work it out. We can work it out.
Life is very short, and there's no time,
for fussing and fighting, my friend,
I have always thought that it's a crime,
so I will ask you once again.
Try to see it my way,
only time will tell if I am right or I am wrong,
while you see it your way,
there's a chance that we may fall apart
before too long.
Life is very short, and there's no time,
for fussing and fighting, my friend,
I have always thought that it's a crime,
so I will ask you one again.
Try to see it my way,
only time will tell if I am right or I am wrong,
while you see it your way,
there's a chance that we may fall apart
before too long.
We can work it out. We can work it out.

›Ich traf ihn auf einem Dorffest in Woolton. Ich war ein pummeliger Schuljunge, und als er einen Arm auf meine Schultern legte, merkte ich, dass er betrunken war. Damals waren wir zwölf, doch trotz seiner Schlagseite kam's dahin, dass wir uns anfreundeten.‹

Paul
über sein erstes
Zusammentreffen mit John

Drive my car

Asked a girl what she wanted to be,
she said, baby can't you see?
I wanna be famous, a star of the screen,
but you can do something in between.
Baby, you can drive my car, yes I'm
gonna be a star,
baby, you can drive my car, and maybe
I'll love you.
I told that girl that my prospects were good,
she said, baby it's understood,
working for peanuts is all very fine,
but I can show you a better time.
Baby, you can drive my car, yes I'm
gonna be a star,
baby, you can drive my car, and maybe
I'll love you.
Beep beep mm, beep beep yeh!
Baby, you can drive my car, yes I'm
gonna be a star,
baby, you can drive my car, and maybe
I'll love you.
I told that girl I could start right away,
and she said, listen, Babe, I've got
something to say,
got no car, and it's breaking my heart,
but I've found a driver, that's a start.
Baby, you can drive my car, yes I'm
gonna be a star,
baby, you can drive my car, and maybe
I'll love you.
Beep beep mm, beep beep yeh!

›Ganz im Gegenteil – ich bin kein Autonarr. Ich werde immer ganz verlegen, wenn ich in eine Werkstätte fahren muss und dann auf den Wagen zeige und sage ›Ich glaub, es ist der … Sie wissen sicher, was ich meine … irgendwas stimmt da nicht.‹‹

Paul

Norwegian wood

I once had a girl,
or I should say
she once had me.
She showed me her room,
isn't it good?
Norwegian wood.
She asked me to stay and she told me to
sit anywhere,
so I looked around and I noticed there
wasn't a chair.
I sat on a rug
biding my time
drinking her wine.
We talked until two,
and then she said,
'It's time for bed'.
She told me she worked in the morning
and started to laugh,
I told her I didn't, and crawled off to
sleep in the bath.
And when I awoke
I was alone
this bird had flown,
so I lit a fire,
isn't it good?
Norwegian wood.

You won't see me

When I call you up your line's engaged.
I have had enough, so act your age,
we have lost the time that was so hard to find,
and I will lose my mind,
if you won't see me, you won't see me.
I don't know why you should want to hide,
but I can't get through my hands are tied,
I won't want to stay I don't have much to say,
but I can turn away,
and you won't see me, you won't see me.
Time after time you refuse to even listen,
I wouldn't mind if I knew what I was missing.
Though the days are few they're filled with tears,
and since I lost you it feels like years,
yes it seems so long girl since you've been gone,
I just can't go on,
if you won't see me, you won't see me.
Time after time you refuse to even listen,
I wouldn't mind if I knew what I was missing.
Though the days are few they're filled with tears,
and since I lost you it feels like years,
yes it seems so long girl since you've been gone,
I just can't go on,
if you won't see me, you won't see me.
Oo – Oo –

Nowhere Man

He's a real Nowhere Man,
sitting in his Nowhere Land,
making all his Nowhere plans for nobody.
Doesn't have a point of view,
knows not where he's going to,
isn't he a bit like you and me?
Nowhere Man please listen,
You don't know what you're missing.
Nowhere Man, the world is at your command.
He's as blind as he can be,
just sees what he wants to see,
Nowhere Man can you see me at all?
Nowhere Man don't worry,
take your time, don't hurry,
leave it all till somebody else,
lends you a hand.
Doesn't have a point of view,
knows not where he's going to,
isn't he a bit like you and me?
Nowhere Man please listen,
You don't know what you're missing.
Nowhere Man, the world is at your command.
He's a real Nowhere Man,
sitting in his Nowhere Land,
making all his Nowhere plans for nobody.
Making all his Nowhere plans for nobody.
Making all his Nowhere plans for nobody.

❛Ich hing so herum und versuchte, mir einen Song einfallen zu lassen, und ich begann an mich selbst zu denken, wie ich so da saß, nichts tat und nicht weiterkam. Als dieser Gedanke gelandet war, war's kinderleicht. Alles kam heraus. Nein, nein… jetzt erinnere ich mich… es war anders. Ich hatte eben aufgehört, mir was auszudenken. Nichts wollte mir einfallen. Ich war sauer und wollte mich ein bisschen aufs Ohr legen. Ich hatte aufgegeben. Dann sah ich mich selbst vor mir sitzen – als Nowhere Man, der in seinem Nowhere Land sitzt.❜

John

Think for yourself

I've got a word or two
to say about the things that you do,
you're telling all those lies,
about the good things that we can have if we close our eyes.
Do what you want to do,
and go where you're going to,
think for yourself,
'cos I won't be there with you.
I left you far behind
the ruins of the life that you had in mind.
And though you still can't see,
I know your mind's made up, you're
gonna cause more misery.
Do what you want to do,
and go where you're going to,
think for yourself,
'cos I won't be there with you.
Although you mind's opaque,
try thinking more,
if just for your own sake.
The future still looks good,
and you've got time to rectify
all the things that you should.
Do what you want to do,
and go where you're going to,
think for yourself,
'cos I won't be there with you.
Think for yourself,
'cos I won't be there with you.

❛Es war einfach eine herrliche Idee von John, eine Eiche zu pflanzen, und die einzige Art, wie man John übertreffen kann, ist, ihn haargenau zu kopieren.❜

Yoko Ono

peter max

The word

Say the word and you'll be free,
Say the word and be like me,
Say the word I'm thinking of,
Have you heard the word is love.
It's so fine, it's sunshine,
it's the word love.
In the beginning I misunderstood,
But now I've got it the word is good.
Say the word and you'll be free,
Say the word and be like me,
Say the word I'm thinking of,
Have you heard the word is love.
It's so fine, it's sunshine,
It's the word love.
Everywhere I go I hear it said,
In the good and the bad books that I have read.
Say the word and you'll be free,
Say the word and be like me,
Say the word I'm thinking of,
Have you heard the word is love.
It's so fine, it's sunshine,
It's the word love.
Now that I know what I feel must be right,
I mean to show ev'rybody the light,
Give the word a chance to say,
That the word is just the way,
It's the word I'm thinking of,
And the only word is love.
It's so fine it's sunshine,
It's the word love.
Say the word love,
Say the word love,
Say the word love,
Say the word love.

„John und ich würden gern Lieder machen, die nur einen einzigen Ton haben – wie damals Long Tall Sally. In The Word waren wir ganz knapp dran. Wär ein hübsches Lied für die Heilsarmee."
Paul

Michelle

Michelle ma belle
These are words that go together well, my
Michelle,
Michelle ma belle,
Sont le mots qui vont tres bien ensemble
tres bien ensemble.
I love you, I love you, I love you,
That's all I want to say,
Until I find a way,
I will say the only words I know that you'll
understand.
Michelle ma belle,
Sont les mots qui vont tres bien ensemble
tres bien ensemble.
I need to, I need to, I need to,
I need to make you see,
oh what you mean to me,
Until I do I'm hoping you will know what I mean.
I love you.
I want you, I want you, I want you,
I think you know by now,
I'll get to you somehow,
Until I do I'm telling you so you'll understand.
Michelle ma belle,
Sont les mots qui vont tres bien ensemble
tres bien ensemble.
I will say the only words I know that you'll
understand,
my Michelle.

What goes on

What goes on in your heart,
what goes on in your mind?
You are tearing me apart,
when you treat me so unkind,
what goes on in your mind?
The other day I saw you,
as I walked along the road,
but when I saw him with you
I could feel my future fold.
It's so easy for a girl like you to lie,
tell me why?
What goes on in your heart,
what goes on in your mind?
You are tearing me apart,
when you treat me so unkind,
what goes on in your mind?
I met you in the morning,
waiting for the tides of time,
but now the tide is turning,
I can see that I was blind.
It's so easy for a girl like you to lie,
tell me why?
What goes on in your heart,
I used to think of no-one else,
but you were just the same,
you didn't even think of me
as someone with a name,
did you mean to break my heart and
watch me die,
tell me why?
What goes on in your heart,
what goes on in your mind?
You are tearing me apart,
when you treat me so unkind,
what goes on in your mind?

“Ich sehnte mich immer danach, Lieder schreiben zu können wie die anderen – und ich hab's auch versucht, aber ich kann das nun mal nicht. Der Text kommt immer ganz hübsch hin, aber so oft ich mir eine Melodie dazu ausdenke und sie dann den anderen vorsinge, sagen sie immer ›jahjah, klingt wie das und das und so und so‹, und wenn sie mir's dann näher erklären, sehe ich ein, was sie meinen. Aber bei einem Lied wurde ich als Mitkomponist erwähnt; es hieß What Goes On.”

Ringo
(Seine erste Eigenkomposition war Don't Pass Me By auf dem Album The Beatles, 1968)

Girl

Is there anybody going to listen to my story,
all about the girl who came to stay?
She's the kind of girl you want so much it makes
you sorry,
still you don't regret a single day.
Ah girl, girl.
When I think of all the times I tried so hard to
leave her,
she will turn to me and start to cry,
and she promises the earth to me and I believe her,
after all this time, I don't know why,
Ah girl, girl.
She's the kind of girl who puts you down,
when friends are there, you feel a fool,
when you say she's looking good,
she acts as if it's understood,
she's cool – oh.
Ah girl, girl.
Was she told when she was young that pain would
lead to pleasure?
Did she understand it when they said
that a man must break his back to earn his day of
leisure,
will she still believe it when he's dead?
Ah girl, girl.

❛Das war ein Song über eine richtige Traumfrau. Früher haben Paul und ich über unsere Texte gelacht, genau wie die Leute aus der Schlagerindustrie. Später haben wir versucht, Text und Musik zu einer Einheit zu machen. Ich mag dieses Lied, es ist eins meiner besten.❜
John

I'm looking through you

I'm looking through you, where did you go?
I thought I knew you, what did I know?
You don't look different, but you have changed,
I'm looking through you, you're not the same.
You lips are moving, I cannot hear,
your voice is soothing but the words aren't clear,
You don't sound different, I've learnt the game,
I'm looking through you, you're not the same.
Why, tell me why did you not treat me right?
Love has a nasty habit of disappearing overnight,
you're thinking of me the same old way,
you were above me, but not today.
The only difference is you're down there.
I'm looking through you and you're nowhere.
Why, tell me why did you not treat me right?
Love has a nasty habit of disappearing overnight,
I'm looking through you, where did you go?
I thought I knew you, what did I know?
You don't look different, but you have changed,
I'm looking through you, you're not the same.
Yeh, I tell you you've changed.

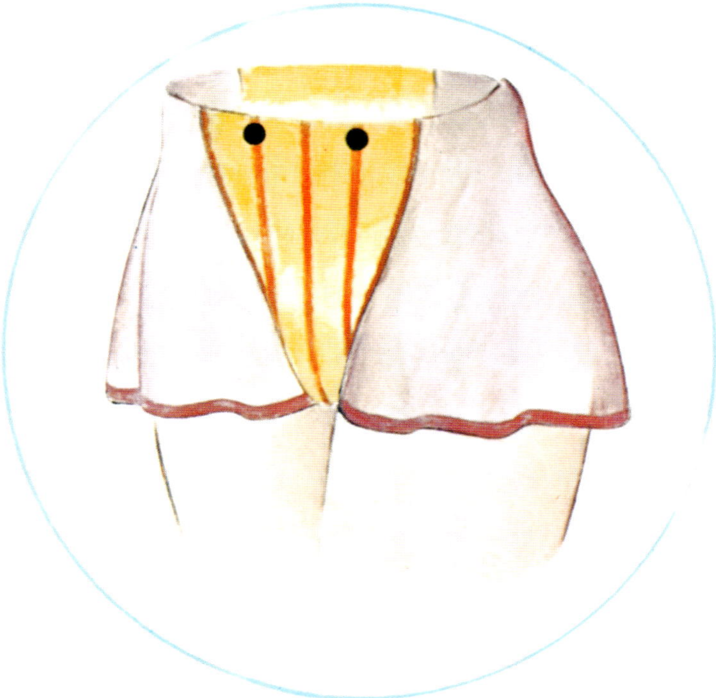

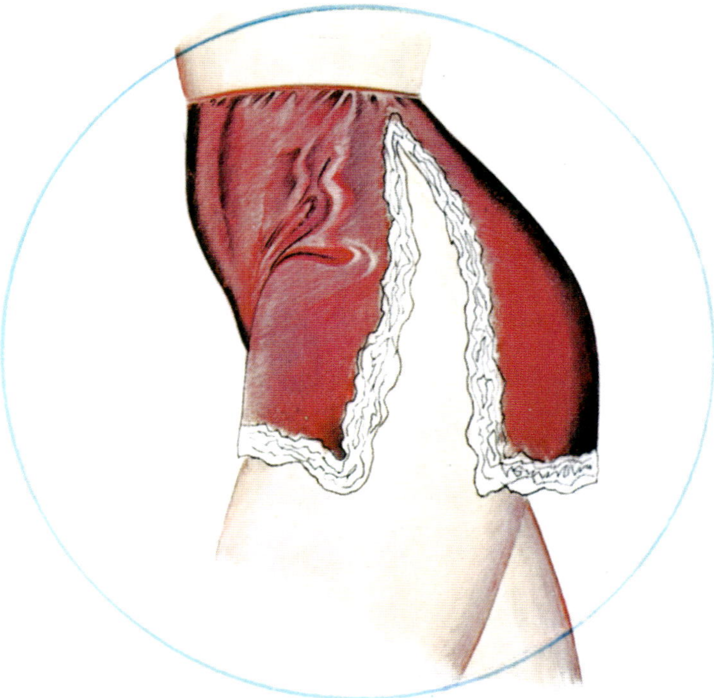

In my life

There are places, I'll remember
all my life, though some have changed,
some forever, not for better,
some have gone and some remain.
All these places had their moments,
with lovers and friends I can still recall,
some are dead and some are living,
in my life I've loved them all.
But of all these friends and lovers,
there is no one compared with you,
and these mem'ries lose their meaning
when I think of love as something new.
Though I know I'll never lose affection
for people and things that went before,
I know I'll often stop and think about them,
in my life I'll love you more.
Though I know I'll never lose affection
for people and things that went before,
I know I'll often stop and think about them
in my life I'll love you more.
In my life I'll love you more.

Wait

It's been a long time, now I'm coming back home,
I've been away now, oh how I've been alone,
wait till I come back to your side,
we'll forget the tears we cried.
But if your heart breaks, don't wait, turn me away,
and if your heart's strong, hold on, I won't delay,
wait till I come back to your side,
we'll forget the tears we cried.
I feel as though you ought to know
that I've been good, as good as I can be,
and if you do, I'll trust in you,
and know that you will wait for me.
It's been a long time, now I'm coming back home,
I've been away now, oh how I've been alone,
wait till I come back to your side,
we'll forget the tears we cried.
I feel as though you ought to know
that I've been good, as good as I can be,
and if you do, I'll trust in you,
and know that you will wait for me.
But if your heart breaks, don't wait, turn me away,
and if your heart's strong, hold on, I won't delay,
wait till I come back to your side,
we'll forget the tears we cried.
It's been a long time, now I'm coming back home,
I've been away now, oh how I've been alone.

Run for your life

I'd rather see you dead, little girl,
than to be with another man.
You'd better keep your head, little girl,
or I won't know where I am.
You'd better run for your life if you can, little girl,
hide your head in the sand, little girl.
Catch you with another man,
that's the end – ah, little girl.
Well you know that I'm a wicked guy
and I was born with a jealous mind,
and I can't spend my whole life tryin',
just to make you toe the line.
You'd better run for your life if you can, little girl,
hide your head in the sand, little girl,
catch you with another man,
that's the end – ah, little girl.
Let this be a sermon,
I mean everything I said,
baby, I'm determined,
and I'd rather see you dead.
You'd better run for your life if you can, little girl,
hide your head in the sand, little girl,
catch you with another man,
that's the end – ah, little girl,
I'd rather see you dead, little girl,
than to be with another man.
You'd better keep your head, little girl,
or I won't know where I am.
You'd better run for your life if you can, little girl,
hide your head in the sand, little girl,
catch you with another man,
that's the end – ah, little girl.

»Ich hab das Lied
nie leiden können.«
John

Woman

Woman do you love me?
Woman if you need me then believe me
I need you to be my woman.
Woman do you love me?
Woman if you need me then believe me
I need you to be my woman.
And should you ask me how I'm doing
what shall I say, things are O.K.
Well I know that they're not
and I still may have lost you.
Woman do you love me?
Woman if you need me then believe me
I need you to be my woman.
And should you take your time and tell me
when we're alone, love will come home
I would give up my world
if you'll say that my girl is my woman.
I've got plenty of time,
help me just to get through it.
Once again you'll be mine
I still think we can do it.
And you know how much I love you.
Woman don't forsake me.
Woman if you take me then believe me
I'll take you to be my woman.

Released by Peter and Gordon, February 1966

»Ich hatte immer mehr Schwierigkeiten beim Schreiben, wenn Yoko dabeisaß. Vielleicht wollte ich bloß etwas ganz Einfaches sagen, zum Beispiel ›Ich liebe dich, Mädchen‹ oder dergleichen, aber wenn Yoko zuschaute, dachte man immer, man müsste etwas ganz Schlaues und Avantgardistisches bringen. Wahrscheinlich hätte sie die einfachen Sachen sogar gemocht, aber sie machte mir Angst.«
Paul

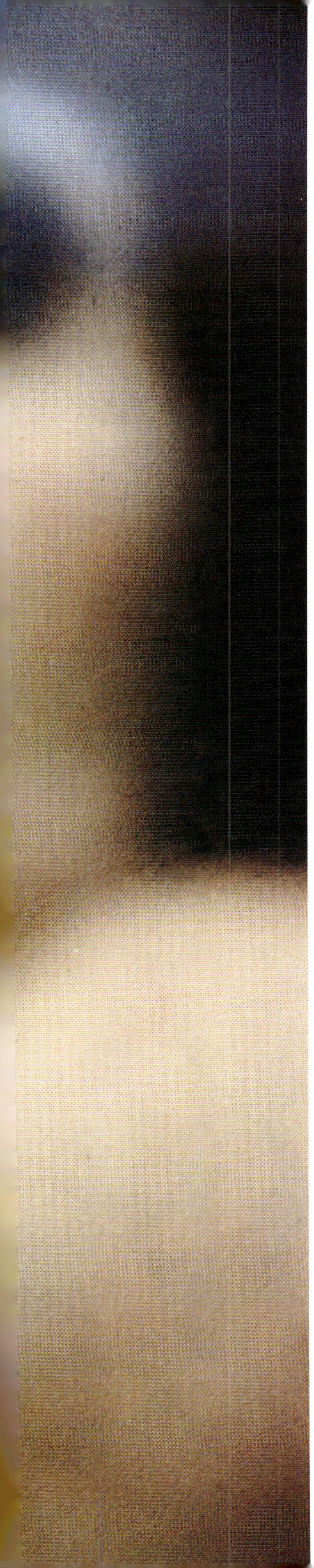

‘Am Schluss hört man, wie ich's verkehrt herum singe. In der Hauptsache hatten wir das Ding schon bei der EMI in den Kasten gebracht, und dann nahmen wir's immer mit nach Hause, um nach einem kleinen Extrascherz zu suchen und das Gitarrensolo durch die Mangel zu drehen. Damals kam ich so um fünf Uhr morgens heim, todmüde, total zugedröhnt, stolperte zu meinem Tonbandgerät, legte das Band ein, doch es lief verkehrt herum, und ich hing ganz berauscht zwischen den Kopfhörern, was ist das bloß, was ist das bloß? Es war das Größte, wissen Sie, und eigentlich wollte ich das ganze Ding verkehrt rum gesungen haben, und das war's dann auch. Wir haben es dann hinten drangeklebt… Reiner Zufall, ich hatte das Band verkehrt eingelegt, die Musik kam einfach verkehrt raus, es machte mich ganz fertig. Die Stimme klingt nach 'nem alten Inder.’

John

Paperback writer

Paperback writer, Paperback writer.
Dear Sir or Madam will you read my book,
It took me years to write will you take a look,
Based on a novel by a man named Lear,
And I need a job,
So I want to be a paperback writer,
Paperback writer.
It's a dirty story of a dirty man,
And his clinging wife doesn't understand.
His son is working for the Daily Mail,
It's a steady job,
But he wants to be a paperback writer,
Paperback writer.
It's a thousand pages give or take a few,
I'll be writing more in a week or two,
I can make it longer if you like the style,
I can change it round,
And I want to be a paperback writer,
Paperback writer.
If you really like it you can have the rights,
It could make a million for you overnight,
If you must return it you can send it here,
But I need a break,
And I want to be a paperback writer,
Paperback writer.

Rain

If the rain comes they run and hide their heads.
They might as well be dead,
If the rain comes, if the rain comes.
When the sun shines they slip in to the shade,
And sip their lemonade,
When the sun shines, when the sun shines.
Rain, I don't mind.
Shine, the weather's fine.
I can show you that when it starts to rain,
Everything's the same,
I can show you, I can show you.
Rain, I don't mind,
Shine, the weather's fine.
Can you hear me that when it rains and shines,
It's just a state of mind,
Can you hear me, can you hear me?

Taxman

Let me tell you how it will be,
There's one for you, nineteen to me,
'Cos I'm the Taxman,
Yeah, I'm the Taxman.
Should five per cent appear too small,
Be thankful I don't take it all,
'Cos I'm the Taxman,
Yeah, I'm the Taxman.
If you drive a car, I'll tax the street,
If you try and sit, I'll tax the seat,
If you get too cold, I'll tax the heat,
If you take a walk, I'll tax your feet.
Taxman.
'Cos I'm the Taxman,
Yeah, I'm the Taxman.
Don't ask me what I want it for
(Taxman Mister Wilson)
If you don't want to pay some more
(Taxman Mister Heath),
'Cos I'm the Taxman,
Yeah, I'm the Taxman.
Now my advice for those who die,
Declare the pennies on your eyes,
'Cos I'm the Taxman,
Yeah, I'm the Taxman.
And you're working for no-one but me,
Taxman.

‘Ich bin schon runter auf meine letzten 50.000 Pfund!’
John

Eleanor Rigby

Ah, look at all the lonely people.
Ah, look at all the lonely people.
Eleanor Rigby picks up the rice in the church where a wedding has been,
lives in a dream.
Waits at the window, wearing a face that she keeps in a jar by the door,
Who is it for?
All the lonely people, where do they all come from?
All the lonely people, where do they all belong?
Father McKenzie, writing the words of a sermon that no-one will hear,
No-one comes near.
Look at him working, darning his socks in the night when there's nobody there,
What does he care?
All the lonely people, where do they all come from?
All the lonely people, where do they all belong?
Ah, look at all the lonely people.
Ah, look at all the lonely people.
Eleanor Rigby died in the church and was buried along with her name.
Nobody came.
Father McKenzie, wiping the dirt from his hands as he walks from the grave.
No-one was saved.
All the lonely people, where do they all come from?
All the lonely people, where do they all belong?

»Zuerst, glaub ich, hieß es Miss Daisy Hawkins – doch ich wollte einen wirklicheren Namen haben, mit mehr Leben drin. Dann kam der Gedanke: ›Eleanor Rigby sammelt den Reis und verträumt ihr Leben‹. Sie hat's nicht geschafft, sie schaffte es niemals bei irgendwem, und sie sah auch nicht danach aus, als würde sie's jemals tun.«

Paul

I'm only sleeping

When I wake up early in the morning,
Lift my head, I'm still yawning.
When I'm in the middle of a dream,
Stay in bed, float up stream (float up stream),
Please don't wake me, no, don't shake me,
Leave me where I am, I'm only sleeping.
Everybody seems to think I'm lazy.
I don't mind, I think they're crazy
Running everywhere at such a speed,
Till they find there's no need (there's no need),
Please don't spoil my day, I'm miles away,
And after all, I'm only sleeping.
Keeping an eye on the world going by my window,
Taking my time, lying there and staring at the ceiling,
Waiting for a sleepy feeling.
Please don't spoil my day, I'm miles away,
And after all, I'm only sleeping.
Keeping an eye on the world going by my window,
Taking my time.
When I wake up early in the morning,
Lift my head, I'm still yawning.
When I'm in the middle of a dream,
Staying in bed, float up stream (float up stream),
Please don't wake me, no, don't shake me,
Leave me where I am, I'm only sleeping.

❛Eigentlich verdanken wir alles unseren Fans. Und natürlich mögen wir sie auch. Aber es gibt eben Zeiten, in denen wir ein bisschen Ruhe haben wollen – und dann können sie ziemlich lästig sein. Aber das gehört wohl dazu.❜
Paul

Love you to

Each day just goes so fast,
I turn around, it's past,
you don't get time to hang a sign on me.
Love me while you can,
before I'm a dead old man.
A life-time is so short,
a new one can't be bought,
but what you've got means such a lot to me.
Make love all day long,
make love singing songs.
Make love all day long,
make love singing songs.
There's people standing round,
who'll screw you in the ground,
they'll fill you in with all their sins,
you'll see.
I'll make love to you,
if you want me to.

❛Ich schrieb mehr und mehr Lieder, als ich mehr Zeit hatte, besonders, als wir mit den Tourneen aufhörten. Nachdem mir die indischen Lieder so sehr durch den Kopf geschwirrt waren, musste das ja wohl kommen.❜
George

Here there and everywhere

To lead a better life, I need my love to be here.
Here, making each day of the year,
changing my life with a wave of her hand.
Nobody can deny that there's something there.
There, running my hands through her hair,
both of us thinking how good it can be.
Someone is speaking but she doesn't know he's
there.
I want her ev'rywhere, and if she's beside me I know
I need never care,
but to love her is to meet her ev'rywhere,
knowing that love is to share,
each one believing that love never dies,
watching her eyes and hoping I'm always there.
I want her ev'rywhere, and if she's beside
me I know I need never care,
but to love her is to meet her ev'rywhere,
knowing that love is to share,
each one believing that love never dies,
watching her eyes and hoping I'm always there.
To be there and ev'rywhere,
here, there and ev'rywhere.

Yellow submarine

In the town where I was born,
lived a man who sailed the sea,
and he told us of his life,
in the land of submarines.
So we sailed on to the sun,
till we found the sea of green,
and we lived beneath the waves,
in our yellow submarine.
We all live in a yellow submarine,
yellow submarine, yellow submarine,
we all live in a yellow submarine,
yellow submarine, yellow submarine.
And our friends are all aboard,
many more of them live next door,
and the band begins to play.
We all live in a yellow submarine,
yellow submarine, yellow submarine,
we all live in a yellow submarine,
yellow submarine, yellow submarine.
As we live a life of ease,
everyone of us has all we need,
sky of blue and sea of green,
in our yellow submarine.
We all live in a yellow submarine,
yellow submarine, yellow submarine,
we all live in a yellow submarine,
yellow submarine, yellow submarine.

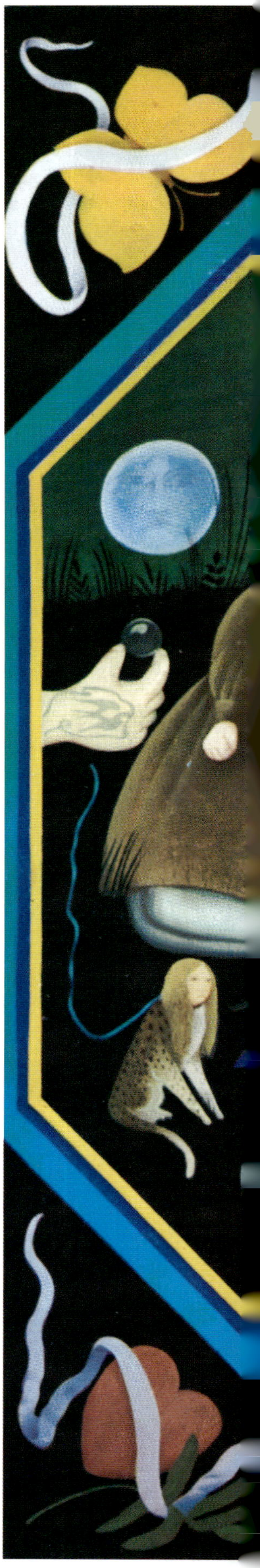

Patrick

“Ich wusste ja, die Leute würden allerlei hineininterpretieren, doch es war schlicht und einfach ein Kinderlied. Ich war ganz verrückt danach, es von kleinen Kindern singen zu lassen.”

Paul zu Yellow Submarine

She said she said

She said I know what it's like to be dead,
I know what it is to be sad,
and she's making me feel like I've never been born.
I said who put all those things in your hair,
things that make me feel that I'm mad,
and you're making me feel like I've never been born.
She said you don't understand what I said,
I said no no no you're wrong, when I was a boy,
ev'rything was right, ev'rything was right.
I said even though you know what you know,
I know that I'm ready to leave,
'cos you're making me feel like I've never been born.
She said you don't understand what I said,
I said no no no you're wrong, when I was a boy,
ev'rything was right, ev'rything was right.
I said even though you know what you know,
I know that I'm ready to leave,
'cos you're making me feel like I've never been born.
She said I know what it's like to be dead,
I know what it is to be sad,
I know what it's like to be dead.

„Das mag ich. Es handelt von einem LSD-Trip, den ich in Los Angeles gemacht habe. Es war der zweite Trip, den wir überhaupt je gemacht haben. Wir hatten davon gehört, und wir wollten gern wissen, was da abgeht. Peter Fonda hat uns besucht und sagte so komische Sachen. ›Ich weiß, wie es ist, wenn man tot ist‹ und so weiter. Also, es hat uns nicht wirklich interessiert, aber er war überhaupt nicht zu bremsen… jedenfalls kommt daher das Lied. Es ist hübsch.“
John

Good day sunshine

Good day sunshine, good day sunshine,
good day sunshine.
I need to laugh, and when the sun is out,
I've got something I can laugh about.
I feel good in a special way,
I'm in love, and it's a sunny day.
Good day sunshine, good day sunshine,
good day sunshine.
We take a walk, the sun is shining down,
burns my feet as they touch the ground.
Good day sunshine, good day sunshine,
good day sunshine.
And then we lie beneath a shady tree,
I love her and she's loving me.
She feels good, she knows she's looking fine,
I'm so proud to know that she is mine.
Good day sunshine, good day sunshine,
good day sunshine.
Good day, good day sunshine.

„Vergessen Sie nicht zu berichten, dass ich strahlte wie ein Honigkuchenpferd.“
Linda Eastman nach der Hochzeit mit Paul zu den Reportern

And your bird can sing

You tell me that you've ev'rything you want,
And your bird can sing,
But you don't get me,
You don't get me.
You say you've seen seven wonders,
And your bird is green,
But you can't see me,
You can't see me.
When your prized possessions start to wear you down,
Look in my direction
I'll be round, I'll be round.
When your bird is broken
will it bring you down?
You may be awoken
I'll be round, I'll be round.
Tell me that you've heard ev'ry sound there is,
and your bird can sing,
But you can't hear me,
You can't hear me.

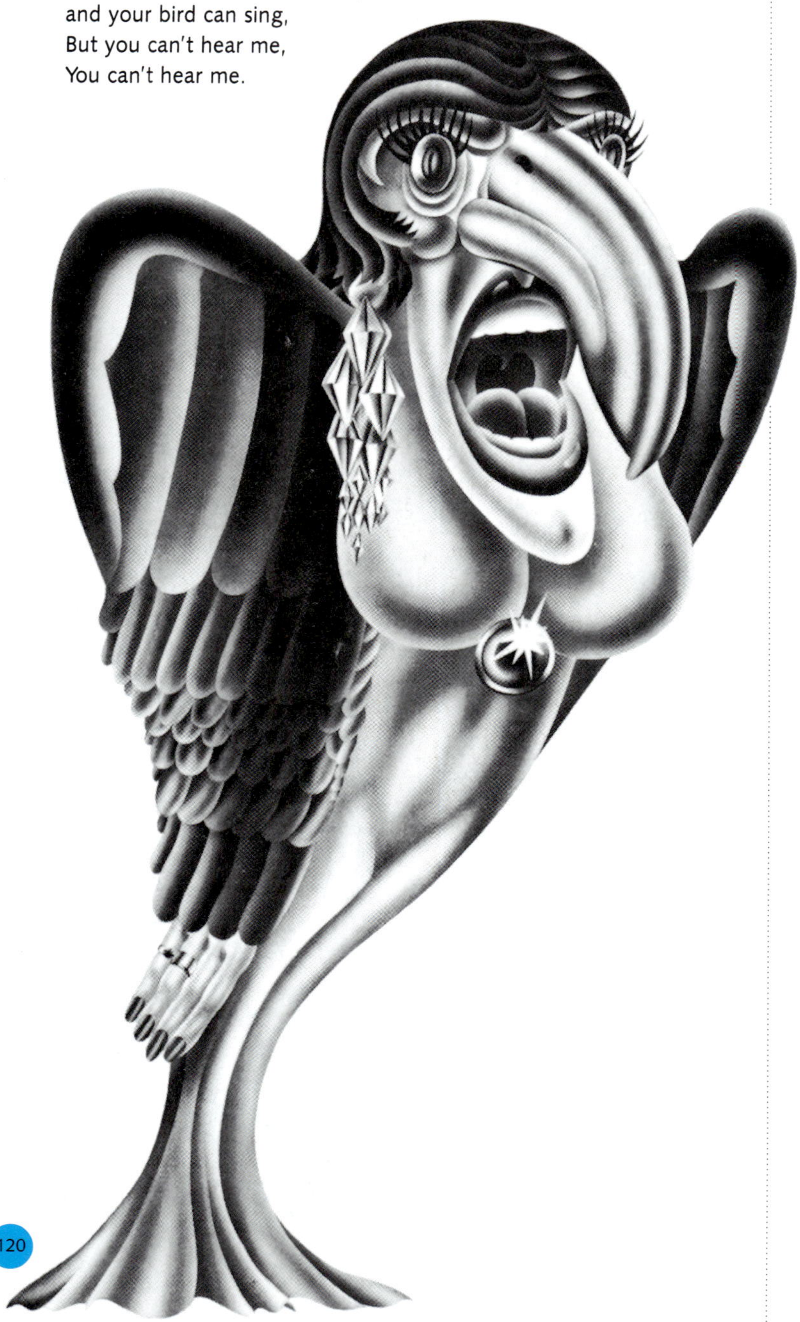

For no one

Your day breaks, your mind aches,
you find that all her words of kindness linger on,
when she no longer needs you.
She wakes up, she makes up,
she takes her time and doesn't feel she has to hu
she no longer needs you.
And in her eyes you see nothing,
no sign of love behind the tears cried for no one
a love that should have lasted years.
You want her, you need her,
and yet you don't believe her,
when she says her love is dead,
you think she needs you.
And in her eyes you see nothing,
no sign of love behind the tears cried for no one
a love that should have lasted years.
You stay home, she goes out,
she says that long ago she knew someone but no
he's gone, she doesn't need him.
Your day breaks, your mind aches,
there will be times when all the things she
said will fill your head,
you won't forget her.
And in her eyes you see nothing,
no sign of love behind the tears cried for no one
A love that should have lasted years.

Doctor Robert

Ring my friend I said you'd call Doctor Robert,
day or night he'll be there anytime at all,
Doctor Robert,
Doctor Robert, you're a new and better man,
he helps you to understand,
he does ev'rything he can, Doctor Robert.
If you are down he'll pick you up, Doctor Robert
take a drink from his special cup, Doctor Robert,
Doctor Robert, he's a man you must believe,
helping ev'ry one in need,
no-one can succeed like Doctor Robert.
Well, well, well, you're feeling fine,
well, well, well, he'll make you, Doctor Robert.
My friend works with the National Health,
Doctor Robert,
don't pay money just to see yourself with
Doctor Robert,
Doctor Robert, you're a new and better man,
he helps you to understand,
he does ev'rything he can, Doctor Robert.
Well, well, well, you're feeling fine,
well, well, well, he'll make you Doctor Robert.
Ring my friend I said you'd call
Doctor Robert.

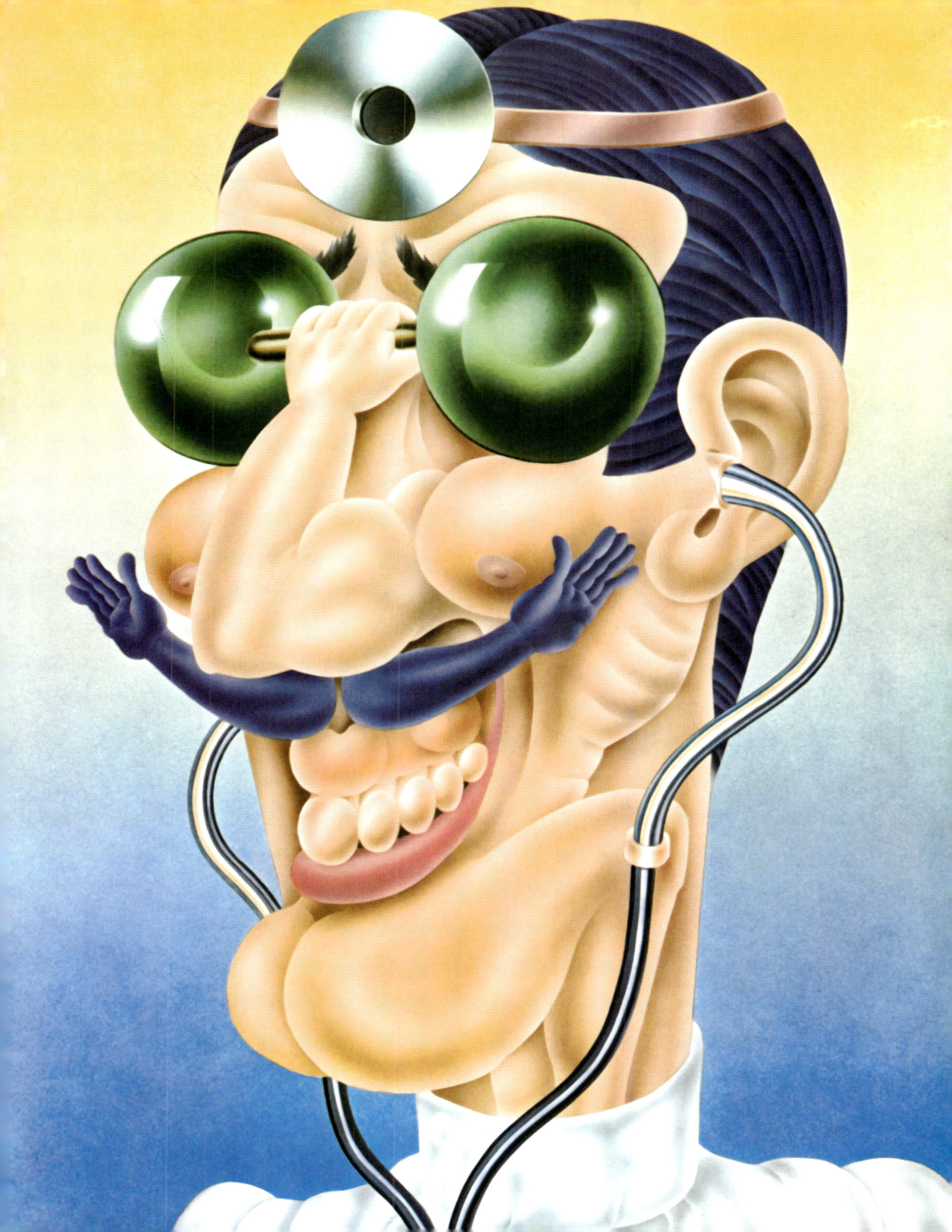

❛ Schließlich sind wir auch nur Menschen. Es tut mir wirklich weh, wenn sie Yoko durch den Kakao ziehen oder sie hässlich nennen und all das Zeug. ❜

John

Got to get you into my life

I was alone, I took a ride,
I didn't know what I would find there.
Another road where maybe I
could see another kind of mind there.
Ooh then I suddenly see you,
ooh did I tell you I need you
ev'ry single day of my life?
You didn't run, you didn't lie,
you knew I wanted just to hold you,
and had you gone, you knew in time
we'd meet again for I had told you.
Ooh you were meant to be near me,
ooh and I want you to hear me,
say we'll be together ev'ry day.
Got to get you into my life.
What can I do, what can I be?
When I'm with you I want to stay there.
If I'm true I'll never leave,
and if I do I know the way there.
Ooh then I suddenly see you,
ooh did I tell you I need you
ev'ry single day of my life?
Got to get you into my life.
Got to get you into my life.
I was alone, I took a ride,
I didn't know what I would find there.
Another road where maybe I
could see another kind of mind there.
Ooh then I suddenly see you,
ooh did I tell you I need you?
ev'ry single day of my life?
What are you doing to my life?

❛Hier wurden wir von dieser Tamla-Motown-Sache beeinflusst. Sie sehen, wir werden durch alles beeinflusst, was gerade läuft.❜
John

I want to tell you

I want to tell you,
my head is filled with things to say,
when you're here,
all those words they seem to slip away.
When I get near to you,
the games begin to drag me down,
it's alright,
I'll make you maybe next time around.
But if I seem to act unkind,
it's only me, it's not my mind,
that is confusing things.
I want to tell you,
I feel hung up and I don't know why,
I don't mind, I could wait for ever,
I've got time.
Sometimes I wish I knew you well,
then I could speak my mind and tell you
maybe you'd understand.
I want to tell you,
I feel hung up and I don't know why,
I don't mind, I could wait for ever,
I've got time. I've got time.

Tomorrow never knows

Turn off your mind relax and float down-stream,
it is not dying, it is not dying,
lay down all thought surrender to the void,
it is shining, it is shining.
That you may see the meaning of within,
it is speaking, it is speaking,
that love is all and love is ev'ryone,
it is knowing, it is knowing.
When ignorance and haste may mourn the dead,
it is believing, it is believing.
But listen to the colour of your dreams,
it is not living, it is not living.
Or play the game existence to the end.
Of the beginning, of the beginning.
Of the beginning. Of the beginning.

Penny Lane

In Penny Lane there is a barber showing photographs
of ev'ry head he's had the pleasure to know.
And all the people that come and go
stop and say 'Hello'.
On the corner is a banker with a motorcar,
the little children laugh at him behind his back.
And the banker never wears a mac
In the pouring rain – very strange.
Penny Lane is in my ears and in my eyes,
there beneath the blue surburban skies
I sit, and meanwhile back
In Penny Lane there is a fireman with an hourglass
and in his pocket is a portrait of the Queen.
He likes to keep his fire engine clean,
it's a clean machine.
Penny Lane is in my ears and in my eyes,
a four of fish and finger pies
in summer meanwhile back
Behind the shelter in the middle of the roundabout
The pretty nurse is selling poppies from a tray.
And though she feels as if she's in a play
she is anyway.
In Penny Lane, the barber shaves another
customer, we see the banker sitting waiting for a trim
and then the fireman rushes in
from the pouring rain – very strange.
Penny Lane is in my ears and in my eyes,
there beneath the blue surburban skies
I sit, and meanwhile back
Penny Lane is in my ears and in my eyes,
there beneath the blue surburban skies …
Penny Lane!

“Penny Lane ist eine Bus-Haltestelle in Liverpool; da gibt's einen Friseurladen mit einem Schaufenster, in dem Fotos mit all den Köpfen zu sehen sind, die der Meister das Vergnügen hatte zu kennen… Ach nein, das ist nicht wahr, es sind nur Fotos mit Frisuren. Aber alle Leute, die vorbeikommen, schauen kurz in den Laden und sagen guten Tag. Es ist teils Wirklichkeit, teils Heimweh nach einem Platz, der ein herrlicher Platz ist, dem blauen Vorstadthimmel, wie wir ihn in Erinnerung haben, und es gibt ihn noch immer.”

Paul

Strawberry Fields forever

Let me take you down,
'cos I'm going to Strawberry Fields.
Nothing is real
and nothing to get hungabout.
Strawberry Fields forever.
Living is easy with eyes closed
Misunderstanding all you see.
It's getting hard to be someone.
But it all works out,
it doesn't matter much to me.
Let me take you down,
'cos I'm going to Strawberry Fields.
Nothing is real
and nothing to get hungabout.
Strawberry Fields forever.
No one I think is in my tree,
I mean it must be high or low.
That is you can't you know tune in.
But it's all right.
That is I think it's not too bad.
Let me take you down,
'cos I'm going to Strawberry Fields.
Nothing is real
and nothing to get hungabout.
Strawberry Fields forever.
Always, no sometimes, think it's me,
but you know I know when it's a dream.
I think I know I mean a 'Yes'.
But it's all wrong.
That is I think I disagree.
Let me take you down,
'cos I'm going to Strawberry Fields.
Nothing is real
and nothing to get hungabout.
Strawberry Fields forever.
Strawberry Fields forever.

“Wissen Sie noch, wie jeder anfing, Beatles-Songs zu analysieren? Bei einigen hab ich auch nie kapiert, worum's dabei gehen sollte.”

Ringo

Sergeant Pepper's Lonely Hearts Club Band

It was twenty years ago today, that
Sergeant Pepper taught the band to play
they've been going in and out of style
but they're guaranteed to raise a smile.
So may I introduce to you
the act you've known for all these years,
Sergeant Pepper's Lonely Hearts Club Band.
We're Sergeant Pepper's Lonely Hearts Club Band,
we hope you will enjoy the show,
We're Sergeant Pepper's Lonely Hearts Club Band,
sit back and let the evening go.
Sergeant Pepper's lonely, Sergeant Pepper's lonely,
Sergeant Pepper's Lonely Hearts Club Band.
It's wonderful to be here,
it's certainly a thrill.
You're such a lovely audience,
we'd like to take you home with us,
we'd love to take you home.
I don't really want to stop the show,
but I thought you might like to know,
that the singer's going to sing a song,
and he wants you all to sing along.
So may I introduce to you
the one and only Billy Shears
and Sergeant Pepper's Lonely Hearts Club Band.

❛Ich dachte einfach an hübsche Worte wie ›Sergeant Pepper‹ und ›Lonely Hearts Club‹, und die kamen ohne besonderen Grund zur gleichen Zeit ihres Weges… Sie sind eine richtige Blaskapelle, aber zugleich auch eine Rock-Band, weil sie diesen Anflug von San Francisco mit dabei haben.❜
Paul

With a little help from my friends

What would you do if I sang out of tune,
would you stand up and walk out on me.
Lend me your ears and I'll sing you a song,
and I'll try not to sing out of key.
I get by with a little help from my friends,
I get high with a little help from my friends,
I'm gonna try with a little help from my friends.
What do I do when my love is away.
(Does it worry you to be alone)
how do I feel by the end of the day
(are you sad because you're on your own)
no I get by with a little help from my friends,
I get high with a little help from my friends,
Oh, I'm gonna try with a little help from my friends.
Do you need anybody,
I need somebody to love.
Could it be anybody
I want somebody to love.
Would you believe in a love at first sight,
yes I'm certain that it happens all the time.
What do you see when you turn out the light,
I can't tell you, but I know it's mine.
Oh I get by with a little help from my friends.
I get high with a little help from my friends,
Oh I'm gonna try with a little help from my friends.
Do you need anybody,
I just need somebody to love,
Could it be anybody,
I want somebody to love.
Oh I get by with a little help from my friends,
Mm I'm gonna try with a little help from my friends,
Oh I get high with a little help from my friends,
Yes I get by with a little help from my friends.

❛Sie wissen ja, ich bin kein aufregender Sänger, weil mein Tonumfang recht bescheiden ist. Deshalb schreiben die Burschen für mich Songs, die schön tief und nicht zu schwierig sind.❜
Ringo

The Beatles

Lucy in the sky with diamonds

Picture yourself in a boat on a river,
with tangerine trees and marmalade skies
Somebody calls you, you answer quite slowly,
a girl with kaleidoscope eyes.
Cellophane flowers of yellow and green,
towering over our head.
Look for the girl with the sun in her eyes,
and she's gone.
Lucy in the sky with diamonds,
Follow her down to a bridge by a fountain
where rocking horse people eat marshmallow pies,
everyone smiles as you drift past the flowers,
that grow so incredibly high.
Newspaper taxis appear on the shore,
waiting to take you away.
Climb in the back with your head in the clouds,
and you're gone.
Lucy in the sky with diamonds,
Picture yourself on a train in a station,
with plasticine porters with looking glass ties,
suddenly someone is there at the turnstile,
the girl with kaleidoscope eyes.
Lucy in the sky with diamonds.

❛Komisch ist das mit dem Lied. Die Leute kamen her und meinten schlau ›jaja, versteh schon – LSD‹, und es war ja auch gerade die Zeit, als die Zeitungen über LSD schrieben, aber daran haben wir nie gedacht. Wie's wirklich war: Johns Sohn Julian hatte in der Schule ein Bild gemalt und er brachte es mit nach Hause, und da gab es ein Mädchen namens Lucy, das mit ihm zur Schule ging. ›Was'n das?‹ fragte John und Julian sagte: ›Lucy am Himmel mit Diamanten.‹❜

Paul

Getting better

It's getting better all the time
I used to get mad at my school
the teachers who taught me weren't cool
Holding me down, turning me round
filling me up with your rules.
I've got to admit it's getting better
It's a little better all the time
I have to admit it's getting better
it's getting better since you've been mine.
Me used to be angry young man
me hiding my head in the sand
You gave me the word
I finally heard
I'm doing the best that I can.
I admit it's getting better
It's a little better all the time yes
I admit it's getting better
it's getting better since you've been mine.
I used to be cruel to my woman
I beat her and kept her apart from the
things that she loved
Man I was mean but I'm changing my scene
and I'm doing the best that I can.
I admit it's getting better
a little better all the time
yes I admit it's getting better
it's getting better since you've been mine.
Getting so much better all the time.

»Als wir in Indien waren, machten alle Pläne, und ich wollte Yoko groß herausbringen, und ich hätt's auch getan, wenn wir uns nicht ineinander verliebt hätten. Es kam eben, wie's kam. Und jetzt sind wir zusammen. Ja, es kam eigentlich viel besser, und es wird immer und immer noch besser…«

John

Fixing a hole

I'm fixing a hole where the rain gets in
and stops my mind from wandering
where it will go.
I'm filling the cracks that ran through the
door
and kept my mind from wandering
where it will go.
And it really doesn't matter if I'm wrong
I'm right
where I belong I'm right
where I belong.
See the people standing there who
disagree and never win
and wonder why they don't get in my
door.
I'm painting my room in a colourful
way
and when my mind is wandering
there I will go.
And it really doesn't matter if I'm wrong
I'm right
where I belong I'm right
where I belong.
Silly people run around they worry me
and never ask me why they don't get past
my door.
I'm taking the time for a number of
things
that weren't important yesterday
and I still go.
I'm fixing a hole where the rain gets in
and stops my mind from wandering
where it will go.

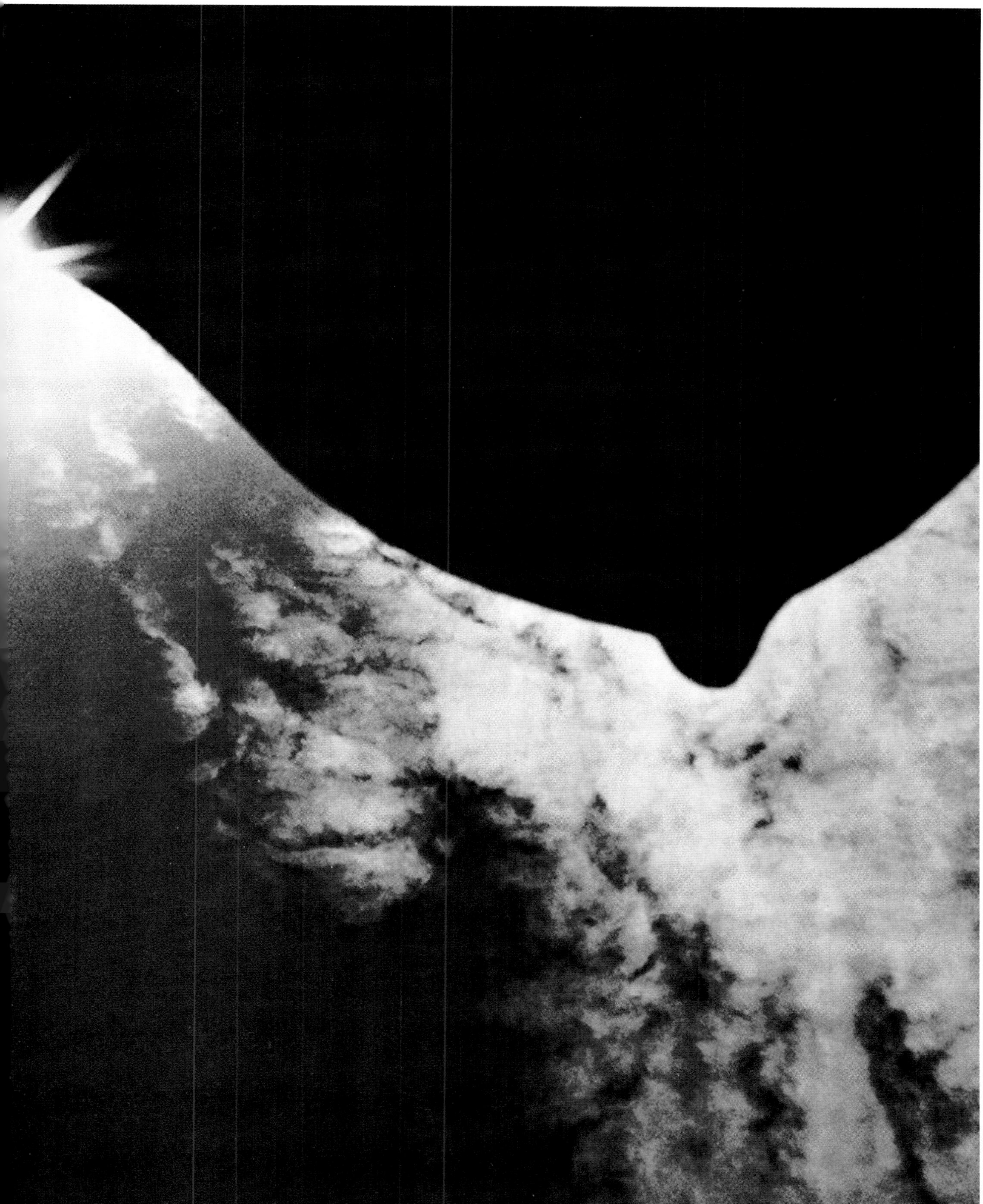

SHE'S LEAVING HOME
WEDNESDAY MORNING AT FIVE O'CLOCK
LATER THAT MORNING
DADDY OUR BABY'S GONE. WHY WOULD SHE TREAT US SO THOUGHTLESSLY. HOW COULD SHE DO THIS TO ME
WE NEVER THOUGHT OF OURSELVES, NEVER A THOUGHT FOR OURSELVES, WE STRUGGLED HARD ALL OUR LIVES TO GET BY.
THE FOLLOWING FRIDAY
CAFE
RESTAURANT
CARS
SHE'S LEAVING HOME BYE BYE BYE
THE EN

She's leaving home

Wednesday morning at five o'clock as the day begins
silently closing her bedroom door
leaving the note that she hoped would say more
she goes downstairs to the kitchen
clutching her handkerchief
quietly turning the backdoor key
stepping outside she is free.
She (We gave her most of our lives)
is leaving (Sacrificed most of our lives)
home (We gave her everything money could buy)
she's leaving home after living alone
for so many years. Bye, bye.
Father snores as his wife gets into her dressing gown
picks up the letter that's lying there
standing alone at the top of the stairs
she breaks down and cries to her husband
daddy our baby's gone.
Why should she treat us so thoughtlessly
how could she do this to me.
She (We never thought of ourselves)
is leaving (We struggled hard all our lives to get by)
she's leaving home after living alone
for so many years. Bye, bye.
Friday morning at nine o'clock she is far away
waiting to keep the appointment she made
meeting a man from the motor trade.
She (What did we do that was wrong)
is leaving (We didn't know it was wrong)
home (Fun is the one thing that money can't buy)
something inside that was always denied
for so many years. Bye, bye.
She's leaving home bye bye.

›Der DAILY MIRROR berichtete über dieses Mädchen, das durchbrannte, und ihr Vater sagte: ›Wir haben ihr alles gegeben, ich hab keine Ahnung, warum sie das getan hat.‹ Aber er gab ihr eben doch nicht so viel, nicht das, was sie haben wollte, als sie fortging.‹

Paul

Being for the benefit of Mr Kite!

For the benefit of Mr. Kite
there will be a show tonight on trampoline.
The Hendersons will all be there
late of Pablo Fanques Fair – what a scene.
Over men and horses hoops and garters
lastly through a hogshead of real fire!
In this way Mr. K. will challenge the world!
The celebrated Mr. K.
performs his feat on Saturday at Bishopsgate
the Hendersons will dance and sing
as Mr. Kite flies through the ring don't be late
Messrs. K. and H. assure the public
their production will be second to none
and of course Henry The Horse dances the waltz!
The band begins at ten to six
when Mr. K. performs his tricks without a sound
and Mr. H. will demonstrate
ten somersaults he'll undertake on solid ground.
Having been some days in preparation
a splendid time is guaranteed for all
and tonight Mr. Kite is topping the bill.

›Bei John hängt dieses alte Plakat, wo ganz oben steht: ›Die Truppe Pablo Fanques präsentiert die Hendersons zugunsten von Mr. Kite‹. Herrlich absurd, das Ganze. Das konnte man nicht erfinden.‹

Paul

Within you without you

We were talking – about the space
between us all
And the people – who hide themselves
behind a wall of illusion
Never glimpse the truth – then it's far too
late – when they pass away.
We were talking – about the love we all
could share – when we find it
to try our best to hold it there – with our love
With our love – we could save the world –
if they only knew.
Try to realise it's all within yourself
no-one else can make you change
And to see you're really only very small,
and life flows on within you and without you.
We were talking – about the love that's
gone so cold and the people,
who gain the world and lose their soul –
they don't know – they can't see – are you
one of them?
When you've seen beyond yourself –
then you may find peace of mind, is
waiting there –
And the time will come when you see
we're all one,
and life flows on within you and without you.

When I'm sixty-four

When I get older losing my hair,
many years from now.
Will you still be sending me a Valentine
birthday greetings bottle of wine.
If I'd been out till quarter to three
would you lock the door.
Will you still need me, will you still feed me,
when I'm sixty-four.
You'll be older too,
and if you say the word,
I could stay with you.
I could be handy, mending a fuse
when your lights have gone.
You can knit a sweater by the fireside
Sunday morning go for a ride.
Doing the garden, digging the weeds,
who could ask for more.
Will you still need me, will you still feed me,
when I'm sixty-four.
Every summer we can rent a cottage,
in the Isle of Wight, if it's not too dear
we shall scrimp and save
grandchildren on your knee
Vera Chuck & Dave
send me a postcard, drop me a line,
stating point of view
indicate precisely what you mean to say
yours sincerely, wasting away
give me your answer, fill in a form
mine for evermore.
Will you still need me, will you still feed me
When I'm sixty-four.

❛Klaus (Voormann, deutscher Musiker bei Manfred Mann) hatte zu Hause ein Harmonium. Ich hatte noch nie auf sowas gespielt. Ich setzte mich davor und dudelte so vor mich hin, um mir die Zeit zu vertreiben, und plötzlich kam Within You, Without You daher. Zuerst kam die Melodie, und dann fing ich den ersten Satz ein. Das Lied entstand aus dem Zeug, das wir an diesem Abend getan hatten.❜
George

METER CHARGES
Monday-Saturday
9.00a.m.-6.00p.m.
6d FOR 1 HOUR
1/-(or 2+6d)FOR 2 HOURS
UNEXPIRED TIME FREE
SUNDAYS AND BANK
HOLIDAYS - NO CHARGE
PENALTY
EXCESS
CHARGE
Coins may be inserted only at time of parking. When the unexpired time or time initially paid for expires, an excess charge of ten shillings must be paid to the Borough Treasurer. To remain after excess period expires renders driver liable to prosecution

Lovely Rita

Lovely Rita meter maid.
Lovely Rita meter maid.
Lovely Rita meter maid.
Nothing can come between us,
when it gets dark I tow your heart away.
Standing by a parking meter,
when I caught a glimpse of Rita,
filling in a ticket in her little white book.
In a cap she looked much older,
and the bag across her shoulder
made her look a little like a military man.
Lovely Rita meter maid,
may I inquire discreetly,
when you are free,
to take some tea with me.
Took her out and tried to win her,
had a laugh and over dinner,
told her I would really like to see her again,
got the bill and Rita paid it,
took her home and nearly made it
sitting on a sofa with a sister or two.
Oh, lovely Rita meter maid,
where would I be without you.
Give us a wink and make me think of you.

‘Ich klimperte in Liverpool auf dem Klavier herum, als jemand mir erzählte, dass die Politessen in Amerika meter maids genannt werden. Ich fand das großartig und ich machte Rita Meter Maid daraus, und ursprünglich sollte es ein Hasslied werden… Doch dann beschloss ich, sie lieb zu haben, und wenn sie auch noch sehr niedlich wär, wie ein Zinnsoldat, mit einer Tasche über der Schulter… Ein Knochenschüttler von Lied, aber ganz nett.’

Paul

Good morning, good morning

Nothing to do to save his life call his wife in
nothing to say but what a day how's your boy been
nothing to do it's up to you
I've got nothing to say but it's O.K.
Good morning, good morning, good morning ...
Going to work don't want to go feeling low down
heading for home you start to roam when you're in
town
everybody knows there's nothing doing
everything is closed it's like a ruin
everyone you see is half asleep.
And you're on your own you're in the street.
Good morning, good morning ...
After a while you start to smile now you feel cool.
Then you decide to take a walk by the old school.
Nothing had changed it's still the same
I've got nothing to say but it's O.K.
Good morning, good morning, good morning ...
People running round it's five o'clock.
Everywhere in town it's getting dark.
Everyone you see is full of life.
It's time for tea and meet the wife.
Somebody needs to know the time, glad that I'm here.
Watching the skirts start to flirt now you're in
gear.
Go to a show you hope she goes.
I've got nothing to say but it's O.K.
Good morning, good morning, good morning ...

»Oft sitze ich am Klavier und arbeite an Liedern, und im Hintergrund läuft leise der Fernseher. Wenn ich nicht so recht bei Laune bin und die Arbeit nicht weitergeht, dann kommen die Worte vom Bildschirm durch. So hörte ich auch Guten Morgen, guten Morgen… Es war ein Werbespot für Corn Flakes.«
John

Sergeant Pepper's Lonely Hearts Club Band (Reprise)

We're Sergeant Pepper's Lonely Hearts Club Band
We hope you have enjoyed the show.
Sergeant Pepper's Lonely Hearts Club Band
We're sorry but it's time to go.
Sergeant Pepper's lonely,
Sergeant Pepper's lonely,
Sergeant Pepper's lonely,
Sergeant Pepper's lonely,
Sergeant Pepper's Lonely Hearts Club Band.
We'd like to thank you once again
Sergeant Pepper's one and only Lonely Hearts Club Band.
It's getting near the end
Sergeant Pepper's lonely
Sergeant Pepper's lonely
Sergeant Pepper's Lonely Hearts Club Band ...

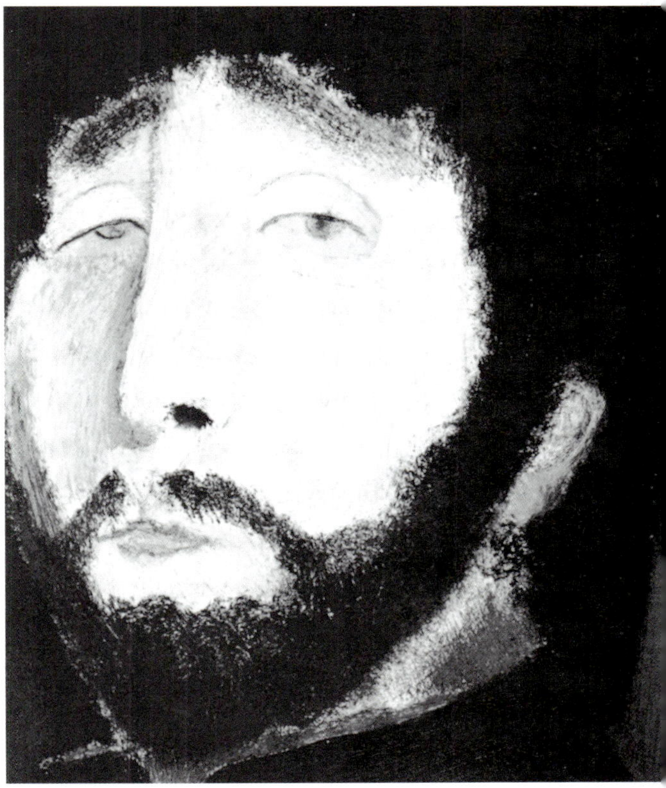

A day in the life

I read the news today oh boy
about a lucky man who made the grade
and though the news was rather sad
well I just had to laugh
I saw the photograph
He blew his mind out in a car
he didn't notice that the lights had changed
a crowd of people stood and stared
they'd seen his face before
nobody was really sure
if he was from the House of Lords.
I saw a film today oh boy
the English Army had just won the war
a crowd of people turned away
but I just had to look
having read the book.
I'd love to turn you on
Woke up, got out of bed,
dragged a comb across my head
found my way downstairs and drank a cup,
and looking up I noticed I was late.
Found my coat and grabbed my hat
made the bus in seconds flat
found my way upstairs and had a smoke,
and somebody spoke and I went into a dream
I heard the news today oh boy
four thousand holes in Blackburn, Lancashire
and though the holes were rather small
they had to count them all
now they know how many holes it takes
to fill the Albert Hall.
I'd love to turn you on.

All you need is love

Love, love, love, love, love, love, love, love, love.
There's nothing you can do that can't be done.
Nothing you can sing that can't be sung.
Nothing you can say but you can learn how to play
the game
It's easy.
There's nothing you can make that can't be made.
No one you can save that can't be saved.
Nothing you can do but you can learn how to be in
time.
It's easy.
All you need is love, all you need is love,
All you need is love, love, love is all you need.
Love, love, love, love, love, love, love, love, love.
All you need is love, all you need is love,
All you need is love, love, love is all you need.
There's nothing you can see that isn't shown.
Nowhere you can be that isn't where you're meant to
be.
It's easy.
All you need is love, all you need is love,
All you need is love, love, love is all you need.
All you need is love (all together now)
All you need is love (everybody)
All you need is love, love, love is all you need.

»Wir werden jedem Staatsmann der Welt zwei Friedenseichen schicken, mit lieben Grüßen von John und Yoko. Wenn sie die Bäumchen pflanzen und zusehen, wie sie wachsen, wird der Gedanke vielleicht in ihre Köpfe gelangen.«
John

Baby you're a rich man

How does it feel to be one of the beautiful people
Now that you know who you are
What do you want to be and have you travelled very far
Far as the eye can see.
How does it feel to be one of the beautiful people
How often have you been there often enough to know
What did you see when you were there nothing that doesn't show
Baby you're a rich man
Baby you're a rich man
Baby you're a rich man too
You keep all your money in a big brown bag inside a zoo
What a thing to do
Baby you're a rich man
Baby you're a rich man
Baby you're a rich man too.
How does it feel to be one of the beautiful people
Tuned to a natural E
Happy to be that way now that you've found another key
What are you going to play
Baby you're a rich man
Baby you're a rich man
Baby you're a rich man too
You keep all your money in a big brown bag inside a zoo
What a thing to do
Baby you're a rich man
Baby you're a rich man
Baby you're a rich man too…

❛Ich möchte Geld haben,
nur um reich zu sein.❜
John

Hello, Goodbye

You say yes, I say no,
You say stop, I say go, go, go.
Oh no.
You say goodbye and I say hello, hello, hello.
I don't know why you say goodbye I say hello, hello, hello.
I don't know why you say goodbye I say hello.
I say high, you say low.
You say why and I say I don't know.
Oh no.
You say goodbye and I say hello, hello, hello.
I don't know why you say goodbye I say hello, hello, hello.
I don't know why you say goodbye I say hello.
Why, why, why, why, why, why, do you
say goodbye, goodbye, bye, bye.
Oh no.
You say goodbye and I say hello, hello, hello.
I don't know why you say goodbye I say hello, hello, hello.
I don't know why you say goodbye I say hello.
You say yes, I say no (I say yes but I may mean no)
You say stop and I say go, go, go (I can stay till it's time to go)
Oh, oh no.
You say goodbye and I say hello, hello, hello.
I don't know why you say goodbye I say hello, hello, hello.
I don't know why you say goodbye I say hello, hello, hello.
I don't know why you say goodbye I say hello, hello, hello.
hello, hello, hello.
hello, hello, hello.
Hela, heba, helloa.

❛Die Herrschaften auf den
billigeren Plätzen bitte
klatschen. Die anderen
klimpern einfach mit ihren
Juwelen.❜
John
bei der Galavorstellung
zu Ehren der Königin

Magical Mystery Tour

Roll up – Roll up for the Mystery Tour.
Roll up, roll up for the Mystery Tour.
(roll up) and that's an invitation
Roll up for the Mystery Tour
(roll up) to make a reservation
Roll up for the Mystery Tour
the Magical Mystery Tour is waiting to take you away
waiting to take you away.
Roll up, roll up for the Mystery Tour.
Roll up, roll up for the Mystery Tour.
(roll up) for the Mystery Tour
(roll up) satisfaction guaranteed
Roll up for the Mystery Tour
the Magical Mystery Tour is hoping to take you away
hoping to take you away now
The Magical Mystery Tour
roll up, roll up for the Mystery Tour.
(roll up) and that's an invitation
Roll up for the Mystery Tour
the Magical Mystery Tour is coming to take you away
coming to take you away
the Magical Mystery Tour is dying to take you away
coming to take you away
the Magical Mystery Tour is dying to take you away
dying to take you away – take you today.

❛Wenn man danach geht, ob es eine gute Unterhaltungssendung für den zweiten Weihnachtstag war – ja, dann haben wir vermutlich einen Bock geschossen. Vater brachte mir heute morgen die schlechten Nachrichten ans Bett wie ein Racheengel. Vielleicht haben die Zeitungen Recht; vielleicht haben wir Recht.❜

Paul
zu den beinahe einhelligen Verrissen des TV-Films Magical Mystery Tour

R. Hausner 1963

I am the walrus

I am he
as you are he
as you are me
and we are all together.
See how they run
like pigs from a gun
see how they fly. I'm crying.
Sitting on a cornflake – waiting for a van to come.
Corporation teeshirt, stupid bloody
Tuesday man you been a naughty boy
you let your face grow long.
I am the eggman oh, they are the eggmen –
Oh I am the walrus GOO GOO G'JOOB.
Mr. City policeman sitting pretty little policeman in a row,
see how they fly
like Lucy in the sky
see how they run. I'm crying – I'm crying I'm crying.
Yellow matter custard dripping from a dead dog's eye.
Crabalocker fishwife pornographic
priestess boy you been a naughty girl,
you let your knickers down.
I am the eggman oh, they are the eggmen -
Oh I am the walrus. GOO GOO G'JOOB.
Sitting on an English garden waiting for the sun,
If the sun don't come, you get a tan from
standing in the English rain.
I am the eggman, oh, they are the eggmen –
Oh I am the walrus. G'JOOB, G'GOO, G'JOOB.
Expert texpert choking smokers
don't they think the joker laughs at you? Ha ha ha!
See how they smile
like pigs in a sty,
see how they snied. I'm crying
Semolina pilchards climbing up the Eiffel Tower.
Elementary penguin singing Hare Khrishna
man you should have seen them
kicking Edgar Allen Poe.
I am the eggman oh, they are the eggmen –
Oh I am the walrus GOO GOO GOO JOOB
GOO GOO GOO JOOB GOO GOO
GOOOOOOOOOOOJOOOOOB.

»Dieses ganze Hin und
Her mit den Aktien…
wie Monopoly.«
John

Your Mother should know

Let's all get up and dance to a song that was a hit
before our Mother was born
Though she was born a long long time ago
your Mother should know – your Mother should know
sing it again.
Lift up your hearts and sing me a song that was a hit
before your Mother was born
Though she was born a long long time ago
your Mother should know – your Mother should know
your Mother should know – your Mother should know
sing it again
Though she was born a long long time ago
your Mother should know – your Mother should know
your Mother should know – your Mother should know
your Mother should know – your Mother should know.

The fool on the hill

Day after day, alone on a hill,
The man with the foolish grin is keeping perfectly still
But nobody wants to know him,
they can see that he's just a fool
and he never gives an answer.
But the fool on the hill sees the sun going down
and the eyes in his head set the world spinning
round.
Well on the way, head in a cloud,
the man of a thousand voices talking perfectly loud.
But nobody ever hears him
or the sound he appears to make
and he never seems to notice.
But the fool on the hill sees the sun going down
and the eyes in his head see the world spinning
round.
And nobody seems to like him,
they can tell what he wants to do
and he never shows his feelings.
But the fool on the hill sees the sun going down
and the eyes in his head see the world spinning
round.
He never listens to them,
he knows that they're the fools.
They don't like him.
The fool on the hill sees the sun going down
and the eyes in his head see the world spinning
round.

»Wir haben einen Fehler gemacht; der Maharishi ist auch nur ein Mensch. Eine Zeit lang dachten wir, er wär's nicht. Wir glauben an die Meditation, aber nicht an den Maharishi und seine Schau. Mit diesem Kapitel sind wir fertig.«
John

Blue Jay Way

There's a fog upon L.A.
And my friends have lost their way
we'll be over soon they said
now they've lost themselves instead.
Please don't be long please don't you be very long
please don't be long or I may be asleep
well it only goes to show
and I told them where to go
ask a policeman on the street
there's so many there to meet
Please don't be long please don't you be very long
please don't be long or I may be asleep
now it's past my bed I know
and I'd really like to go
soon will be the break of day
sitting here in Blue Jay Way
Please don't be long please don't you be very long
please don't be long or I may be asleep
Please don't be long please don't you be very long
please don't be long
Please don't be long please don't you be very long
please don't be long
Please don't be long please don't you be very long
please don't be long
don't be long – don't be long – don't be long
don't be long – don't be long – don't be long

»Derek wurde aufgehalten. Er rief an und sagte, er würde sich verspäten. Ich sagte ihm am Telefon, das Haus sei in Blue Jay Way. Er sagte, er würde es schon finden, er könne immer noch einen Polizisten fragen.«
George

Lady Madonna

Lady Madonna children at your feet
wonder how you manage to make ends meet.
Who finds the money when you pay the rent?
Did you think that money was heaven sent?
Friday night arrives without a suitcase
Sunday morning creep in like a nun
Monday's child has learned to tie his bootlace.
See how they'll run.
Lady Madonna baby at your breast
wonder how you manage to feed the rest.
See how they'll run.
Lady Madonna lying on the bed
listen to the music playing in your head.
Tuesday afternoon is never ending
Wednesday morning papers didn't come
Thursday night your stockings needed mending.
See how they'll run.
Lady Madonna children at your feet
wonder how you manage to make ends meet.

The inner light

Without going out of my door
I can know all things on earth.
Without looking out of my window
I could know the ways of heaven.
The farther one travels,
The less one knows,
The less one knows.
Without going out of your door
You can know all things on earth.
Without looking out of your window
You can know the ways of heaven.
The farther one travels,
The less one knows,
The less one knows.
Arrive without travelling.
See all without looking.
(See all without looking).

»George hat es geschrieben. Vergesst die indische Musik und hört euch die Melodie an. Ist es nicht eine schöne Melodie? Sie ist fantastisch, bei Gott.«
Paul

Step inside love

Step inside love, let me find you a place,
where the cares of the day will be carried away
by the smile on your face.
We are together now and forever, come my way.
Step inside love and stay.
Step inside love, step inside love, step inside love.
I want you to stay.
You look tired love, let me turn down the light
come in out of the cold, rest your head on my
shoulder
and love me tonight.
I'll always be here if you should need me,
night and day.
Step inside love and stay.
Step inside love, step inside love,
I want you to stay.
When you leave me, say you'll see me again,
for I'll know in my heart we will not be apart
and I'll miss you till then.
We'll be together now and forever, come my way.
Step inside love and stay.
Step inside love (I want you to).
Step inside love (I know you do).
I want you to stay.

Released by Cilla Black, March 1968

III

The Apple Years
1968→1970

Hey Jude

Hey Jude don't make it bad,
take a sad song and make it better,
remember, to let her into your heart,
then you can start to make it better.
Hey Jude don't be afraid,
you were made to go out and get her,
the minute you let her under your skin,
then you begin to make it better.
And anytime you feel the pain,
Hey Jude refrain,
don't carry the world upon your shoulders.
For well you know that it's a fool,
who plays it cool,
by making his world a little colder.
Hey Jude don't let me down,
you have found her now go and get her,
remember (Hey Jude) to let her into your heart,
then you can start to make it better.
So let in out and let it in
Hey Jude begin,
you're waiting for someone to perform with.
And don't you know that it's just you.
Hey Jude, you'll do,
the movement you need is on your shoulder.
Hey Jude, don't make it bad,
take a sad song and make it better,
remember to let her under your skin,
then you'll begin to make it better.

❛Eigentlich sollte es Hey Jules heißen, doch es kam anders. Ich fuhr runter nach Weybridge, um Cynthia (Lennon) und Julian zu besuchen, und ich fing an zu singen ›Hey Jules, mach keinen Mist‹, und dann machte ich Hey Jude daraus. So geht das eben manchmal.❜

Paul

Back in the USSR

Flew in from Miami Beach BOAC.
Didn't get to bed last night.
On the way the paper bag was on my knee.
Man I had a dreadful flight.
I'm back in the USSR.
You don't know how lucky you are boy
Back in the USSR.
Been away so long I hardly knew the place.
Gee it's good to be back home.
Leave it till tomorrow to unpack my case.
Honey disconnect the phone.
I'm back in the USSR.
You don't know how lucky you are boy
Back in the US. Back in the US. Back in
the USSR.
Well the Ukraine girls really knock me out.
They leave the West behind.
And Moscow girls make me sing and shout
That Georgia's always on my mind.
I'm back in the USSR.
You don't know how lucky you are boys
Back in the USSR.
Show me round your snow peaked mountains way
down south
Take me to your daddy's farm
Let me hear your balalaikas ringing out
Come and keep your comrade warm.
I'm back in the USSR.
You don't know how lucky you are boys
Back in the USSR.

Revolution

You say you want a revolution
Well, you know
we all want to change the world.
You tell me that it's evolution,
Well, you know
we all want to change the world.
But when you talk about destruction,
Don't you know that you can count me out.
Don't you know that it's going to be alright,
Alright, alright.
You say you got a real solution
Well, you know
we'd all love to see the plan.
You ask me for a contribution,
Well, you know
we're doing what we can.
But if you want money for people with minds that
hate,
All I can tell you is brother you have to wait.
Don't you know it's going to be alright,
Alright, alright.
You say you'll change a constitution
well, you know
we all want to change your head.
You tell me it's the institution,
well, you know
you better free your mind instead.
But if you go carrying pictures of Chairman Mao,
You ain't going to make it with anyone anyhow.
Don't you know it's going to be alright,
alright, alright.

❛Viele von den Leuten, die sich bitter darüber beklagten, dass man uns den M.B.E. verliehen hat, haben ihren für Heldentaten im Krieg bekommen – dafür, dass sie andere Menschen umgelegt haben. Wir haben unseren gekriegt, weil wir die Menschen unterhalten. Wir verdienen unseren Orden eher, finde ich. Sie nicht auch?❜

John

peter max

Dear Prudence

Dear Prudence, won't you come out to play.
Dear Prudence, greet the brand new day.
The sun is up, the sky is blue.
It's beautiful and so are you.
Dear Prudence won't you come out to play?
Dear Prudence open up your eyes.
Dear Prudence see the sunny skies.
The wind is low the birds will sing
That you are part of everything.
Dear Prudence won't you open up your eyes?
Look around round
Look around round round
Look around.
Dear Prudence let me see you smile.
Dear Prudence like a little child.
The clouds will be a daisy chain.
So let me see you smile again.
Dear Prudence won't you let me see you smile?

Glass onion

I told you about Strawberry Fields.
You know the place where nothing is real.
Well here's another place you can go
Where everything flows.
Looking through the bent-backed tulips
To see how the other half live
Looking through a glass onion.
I told you about the walrus and me – man.
You know that we're as close as can be – man.
Well here's another clue for you all
The walrus was Paul.
Standing on the cast iron shore – yeah.
Lady Madonna trying to make ends meet – yeah.
Looking through a glass onion.
Oh yeah oh yeah oh yeah
Looking through a glass onion.
I told you about the fool on the hill.
I tell you man he living there still.
Well here's another place you can be. Listen to me.
Fixing a hole in the ocean
Trying to make a dove-tail joint – yeah
Looking through a glass onion.

Ob-la-di, ob-la-da

Desmond has a barrow in the market place.
Molly is a singer in a band.
Desmond says to Molly – girl I like your face
And Molly says this as she takes him by the hand.
Ob-la-di ob-la-da life goes on bra
La-la how the life goes on
Ob-la-di ob-la-da life goes on bra
La-la how the life goes on
Desmond takes a trolley to the jewellers
stores,
Buys a twenty carat golden ring.
Takes it back to Molly waiting at the door
And as he gives it to her she begins to sing
In a couple of years they have built
A home sweet home
With a couple of kids running in the yard
Of Desmond and Molly Jones.
Happy ever after in the market place
Desmond lets the children lend a hand.
Molly stays at home and does her pretty face
And in the evening she still sings it with the band.
Happy ever after in the market place
Molly lets the children lend a hand.
Desmond stays at home and does his pretty face
And in the evening she's a singer with the band.
And if you want some fun – take Ob-la-di Ob-la-da.

Wild honey pie

Honey pie
Honey pie
Honey pie
Honey pie hello ….

❛Das war nur so ein Fragment von einem Instrumental, bei dem wir uns unsicher waren. Aber Patti mochte es sehr, und da ist es auf dem Album geblieben.❜
Paul

The continuing story of Bungalow Bill

Hey, Bungalow Bill
what did you kill
Bungalow Bill?
He went out tiger hunting with his elephant and gun.
In case of accidents he always took his mom.
He's the all American bullet-headed saxon mother's son.
All the children sing
Hey, Bungalow Bill
What did you kill
Bungalow Bill?
Deep in the jungle where the mighty tiger lies
Bill and his elephants were taken by surprise.
So Captain Marvel zapped in right between the eyes.
All the children sing
Hey, Bungalow Bill
What did you kill
Bungalow Bill?
The children asked him if to kill was not a sin.
Not when he looked so fierce, his mother butted in.
If looks could kill it would have been us
instead of him.
All the children sing
Hey, Bungalow Bill
What did you kill
Bungalow Bill?

❛Das Schlimme ist ja, dass im Pop- und im Schallplatten-Geschäft so viele Leute am Drücker sitzen, die keine Ahnung davon haben.❜
Paul

chwast

Happiness is a warm gun

She's not a girl who misses much.
Do do do do do do do do
She's well acquainted with the touch of
the velvet hand
Like a lizard on a window pane.
The man in the crowd with the
multicoloured mirrors
On his hobnail boots
Lying with his eyes while his hands are busy
Working overtime
A soap impression of his wife which he ate
And donated to the National Trust.
I need a fix 'cause I'm going down.
Down to the bits that I left uptown.
I need fix 'cause I'm going down.
Mother Superior jump the gun
Mother Superior jump the gun
Mother Superior jump the gun
Mother Superior jump the gun
Happiness is a warm gun
Happiness is a warm gun
When I hold you in my arms
And I feel my finger on your trigger
I know no one can do me no harm
because happiness is a warm gun.
Yes it is.

›Ich würd sagen, mein Lieblingslied auf dem Album The Beatles.‹
Paul

Martha my dear

Martha my dear though I spend my days
in conversation
Please
Remember me Martha my love
Don't forget me Martha my dear
Hold your head up you silly girl look what
you've done
When you find yourself in the thick of it
Help yourself to a bit of what is all around you
Silly girl.
Take a good look around you
Take a good look you're bound to see
That you and me were meant to be for each other
Silly girl.
Hold your hand out you silly girl see what you've
done
When you find yourself in the thick of it
Help yourself to a bit of what is all around you
Silly girl.
Martha my dear you have always been
my inspiration
Please
Be good to me Martha my love
Don't forget me Martha my dear.

I'm so tired

I'm so tired, I haven't sleep a wink,
I'm so tired, my mind is on the blink.
I wonder should I get up and fix myself a
drink.
No, no, no.
I'm so tired I don't know what to do.
I'm so tired my mind is set on you.
I wonder should I call you but I know
what you'd do.
You'd say I'm putting you on.
But it's no joke, it's doing me harm.
You know I can't sleep, I can't stop my
brain
You know it's three weeks, I'm going
insane.
You know I'd give you everything I've got
for a little peace of mind.
I'm so tired, I'm feeling so upset
Although I'm so tired I'll have another cigarette
And curse Sir Walter Raleigh
He was such a stupid git.

»Reiner Mord, diese Tourneen. Von Amerika sahen wir so gut wie nichts, weil wir die ganze Zeit in Hotelzimmern bleiben mussten. Und immer waren wir wie erschlagen vor Müdigkeit.«
Ringo

Blackbird

Blackbird singing in the dead of night
Take these broken wings and learn to fly.
All your life
You were only waiting for this moment to arise.
Blackbird singing in the dead of night
Take these sunken eyes and learn to see.
All your life
You were only waiting for this moment to be free.
Blackbird fly, Blackbird fly
Into the light of the dark black night.
Blackbird fly, Blackbird fly
Into the light of the dark black night.
Blackbird singing in the dead of night
Take these broken wings and learn to fly.
All your life
You were only waiting for this moment to arise
You were only waiting for this moment to arise
You were only waiting for this moment to arise

Rocky Raccoon

Now somewhere in the black mountain hills of
Dakota
There lived a young boy named Rocky Raccoon.
And one day his woman ran off with another guy.
Hit young Rocky in the eye Rocky didn't like that.
He said I'm gonna get that boy.
So one day he walked into town
Booked himself a room in the local saloon.
Rocky Raccoon checked into his room
Only to find Gideon's Bible.
Rocky has come equipped with a gun
To shoot off the legs of his rival.
His rival it seems had broken his dreams
By stealing the girl of his fancy.
Her name is Magill and she called herself Lill
but everyone knew her as Nancy.
Now she and her man who called himself Dan
Were in the next room at the hoe down.
Rocky bust in and grinning a grin.
He said Danny boy this is a showdown
But Daniel was hot – he drew first and shot
And Rocky collapsed in the corner.
Now the doctor came in stinking of gin
And proceeded to lie on the table.
He said Rocky you met your match.
And Rocky said, Doc it's only a scratch
And I'll be better, I'll be better doc as
soon as I am able.
Now Rocky Raccoon he fell back in his room
Only to find Gideon's Bible.
Gideon checked out and he left in no doubt
To help with good Rocky's revival.

WHY DON'T WE D-DO IT IN THE ROAD?.....
WHY DON'T WE DO IT IN THE ROAD?.....
WHY DON'T WE DO IT IN THE ROAD?.....
WHY DON'T WE DO IT IN THE ROAD?.....
NO ONE WILL BE WATCHING US...
WHY DON'T WE DO IT IN THE ROAD!!!
why did they do it in the road?...
WHY DON'T WE DO IT IN THE ROAD?.....
they got no sense, they should have knowed
WHY DON'T WE DO IT IN THE ROAD?.....
why did they do it in the road?.....
WHY DON'T WE DO IT IN THE ROAD?
right where the dumptruck dropped its' load....
WHY DON'T WE DO IT IN THE ROAD?.....
the driver did not see them there...
NO ONE WILL BE WATCHING US...
oh why did they do it in the road???
WHY DON'T WE DO IT IN THE ROAD?
HIGHWAY 1
WHY DON'T WE DO IT IN THE ROAD?
NO ONE WILL BE WATCHING US..
WHY DON'T WE DO IT IN THE ROAD?
WHY DON'T WE DO IT IN THE ROAD?
WHY DON'T WE DO IT IN THE ROAD?
WHY DON'T WE DO IT IN THE ROAD?
RICK GRIFFIN 1969

Why don't we do it in the road?

Why don't we do it in the road?
No one will be watching us.
Why don't we do it in the road?

I will

Who knows how long I've loved you.
You know I love you still.
Will I wait a lonely lifetime
If you want me to – I will.
For if I ever saw you
I didn't catch your name.
But it never really mattered
I will always feel the same.
Love you forever and forever.
Love you with all my heart.
Love you whenever we're together.
Love you when we're apart.
And when at last I find you
Your song will fill the air.
Sing it loud so I can hear you.
Make it easy to be near you
For the things you do endear you to me
You know I will.
I will.

❛Ich merkte, dass sie mir schon ziemlich lang durch den Kopf ging. Wir haben lange Zeit über das Heiraten geredet. Schließlich beschlossen wir, es zu tun, anstatt darüber zu reden. Linda hat's recht schnell geschafft.❜
Paul

Julia

Half of what I say is meaningless
But I say it just to reach you, Julia.
Julia, Julia, oceanchild, calls me
So I sing a song of love, Julia
Julia, seashell eyes, windy smile, calls me
So I sing a song of love, Julia.
Her hair of floating sky is shimmering,
glimmering,
In the sun.
Julia, Julia, morning moon, touch me
So I sing a song of love, Julia.
When I cannot sing my heart
I can only speak my mind, Julia.
Julia, sleeping sand, silent cloud, touch me
So I sing a song of love, Julia.
Hum hum hum hum … calls me
So I sing a song of love for Julia, Julia, Julia.

»Am Tag der Premiere von Yeah Yeah Yeah wurde ich zweiundsechzig, und wir gingen alle ins Dorchester. Paul gab mir ein großes Paket. Ich öffnete es, und es war ein Bild von einem Pferd. ›Sehr hübsch‹, sagte ich. Aber was, dachte ich, fang' ich an mit einem Bild von einem Pferd? Paul muss mein Gesicht gesehen haben, denn er sagte: ›Nicht nur irgendein Bild, Papa. Ich hab' dir das verdammte Pferd gekauft.‹«
James McCartney

Birthday

You say it's your birthday.
It's my birthday too – yeah.
They say it's your birthday.
We're gonna have a good time.
I'm glad it's your birthday
Happy birthday to you.
Yes we're going to a party party
Yes we're going to a party party
Yes we're going to a party party.
I would like you to dance – Birthday
Take a cha-cha-cha-chance – Birthday
I would like you to dance – Birthday dance
You say it's your birthday.
It's my birthday too – yeah.
You say it's your birthday.
We're gonna have a good time.
I'm glad it's your birthday
Happy birthday to you.

Yer blues

Yes I'm lonely wanna die
Yes I'm lonely wanna die.
If I ain' t dead already.
Ooh girl you know the reason why.
In the morning wanna die.
In the evening wanna die.
If I ain't dead already.
Ooh girl you know the reason why.
My mother was of the sky.
My father was of the earth.
But I am of the universe
And you know what it's worth.
I'm lonely wanna die.
If I ain't dead already.
Ooh girl you know the reason why.
The eagle picks my eye.
The worm he licks my bone.
I feel so suicidal
Just like Dylan's Mr. Jones.
Lonely wanna die.
If I ain't dead already.
Ooh girl you know the reason why.
Black cloud crossed my mind.
Blue mist round my soul.
Feel so suicidal
Even hate my rock and roll.
Wanna die yeah wanna die.
If I ain't dead already.
Ooh girl you know the reason why.

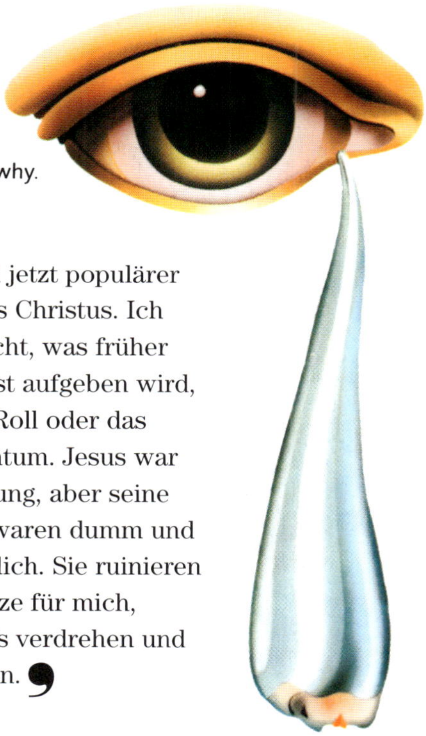

»Wir sind jetzt populärer als Jesus Christus. Ich weiß nicht, was früher den Geist aufgeben wird, Rock'n'Roll oder das Christentum. Jesus war in Ordnung, aber seine Jünger waren dumm und gewöhnlich. Sie ruinieren das Ganze für mich, weil sie's verdrehen und verzerren.«
John

Mother Nature's son

Born a poor young country boy –
Mother Nature's son.
All day long I'm sitting singing songs
for everyone.
Sit beside a mountain stream – see her waters rise.
Listen to the pretty sound of music as she flies.
Find me in my field of grass –
Mother Nature's son.
Swaying daisies sing a lazy song beneath the sun.
Mother Nature's son.

»Ich hab nie ernstlich was dazu getan, um es so kommen zu lassen. Es schafft sich selbst. Ich bin hier, weil es so gekommen ist, das ist alles. Doch ich hab nicht mehr dazu getan, um es geschehen zu lassen, als ›ja‹ gesagt.«
Ringo

Everybody's got something to hide except for me and my monkey

Come on come on come on come on
Come on is such a joy
Come on is such a joy
Come on take it easy
Come on take it easy.
Take it easy take it easy.
Everybody's got something to hide except for me
and my monkey.
The deeper you go the higher you fly.
The higher you fly the deeper you go.
So come on come on
Come on is such a joy
Come on take it easy
Come on take it easy.
Take it easy take it easy.
Everybody's got something to hide except for me
and my monkey.
Your inside is out and your outside is in.
Your outside is in and your inside is out.
So come on come on
Come on is such a joy
Come on is such a joy
Come on take it easy
Come on take it easy.
Take it easy take it easy.
Everybody's got something to hide except for me
and my monkey.

“Ich bin sehr schüchtern.
John ist auch schüchtern.”
Yoko Ono

Sexy Sadie

Sexy Sadie what have you done.
You made a fool of everyone.
You made a fool of everyone.
Sexy Sadie ooh what have you done.
Sexy Sadie you broke the rules.
You layed it down for all to see.
You layed it down for all to see.
Sexy Sadie ooh you broke the rules.
One sunny day the world was waiting for a lover.
She came along to turn on everyone.
Sexy Sadie the greatest of them all.
Sexy Sadie how did you know.
The world was waiting just for you.
The world was waiting just for you.
Sexy Sadie oooh how did you know.
Sexy Sadie you'll get yours yet.
However big you think you are.
However big you think you are.
Sexy Sadie ooh you'll get yours yet.
We gave her everything we owned just to
sit at her table
Just a smile would lighten everything
Sexy Sadie she's the latest and the greatest of
them all.
She made a fool of everyone
Sexy Sadie.
However big you think you are
Sexy Sadie.

Helter skelter

When I get to the bottom I go back to the
top of the slide
Where I stop and I turn and I go for a ride
till I get to the bottom and I see you again.
Do you, don't you want me to love you.
I'm coming down fast but I'm miles above you.
Tell me tell me tell me come on tell me the answer.
You may be a lover but you ain't no dancer.
Helter skelter helter skelter
Helter skelter.
Will you, won't you want me to make you.
I'm coming down fast but don't let me break you.
Tell me tell me tell me the answer.
You may be a lover but you ain't no dancer.
Look out helter skelter helter skelter
Helter skelter
Look out, 'cause here she comes.
When I get to the bottom I go back to the
top of the slide
Where I stop and I turn and I go for a ride
And I get to the bottom and I see you again.
Well do you, don't you want me to make you.
I'm coming down fast but don't let me break you.
Tell me tell me tell me the answer.
You may be a lover but you ain't no dancer.
Look out helter skelter helter skelter
Helter skelter
Look out helter skelter
She's coming down fast
Yes she is yes she is.

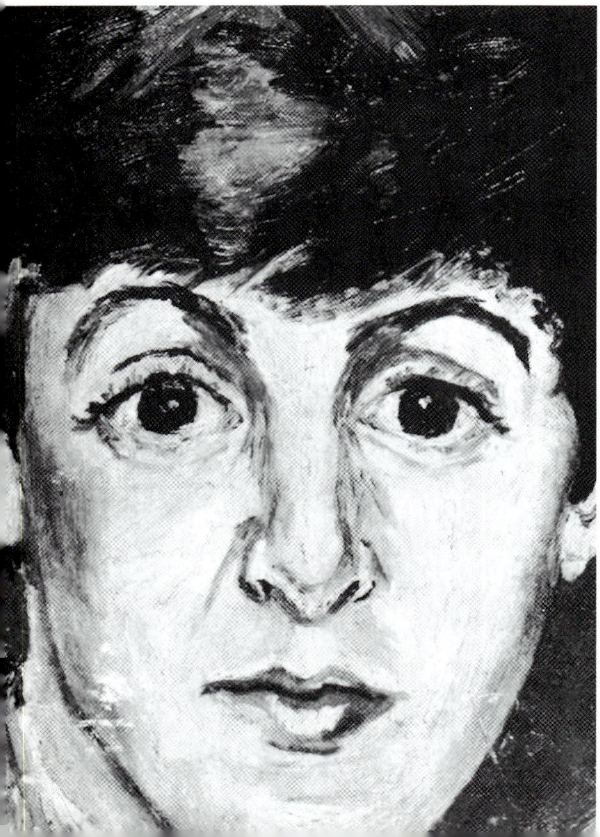

Honey pie

She was a working girl
North of England way.
Now she's hit the big time
In the USA.
And if she could only hear me
This is what I'd say.
Honey pie you are making me crazy.
I'm in love but I'm lazy.
So won't you please come home.
Oh honey pie my position is tragic.
Come and show me the magic
of your Hollywood Song.
You became a legend of the silver screen
And now the thought of meeting you
Makes me weak in the knee.
Oh honey pie you are driving me frantic.
Sail across the Atlantic
To be where you belong.
Will the wind that blew her boat
Across the sea
Kindly send her sailing back to me.
Honey pie you are making me crazy.
I'm in love but I'm lazy.
So won't you please come home.

“Ich glaube, für die Leute
bin ich der Niedliche.”
Paul

Cry baby cry

Cry baby cry.
Make your mother sigh.
She's old enough to know better.
The king of Marigold was in the kitchen
Cooking breakfast for the queen.
The queen was in the parlour
Playing piano for the children of the king.
Cry baby cry.
Make your mother sigh.
She's old enough to know better. So cry baby cry.
The king was in the garden
Picking flowers for a friend who came to play.
The queen was in the playroom
Painting pictures for the children's holiday.
Cry baby cry.
Make your mother sigh.
She's old enough to know better. So cry baby cry.
The duchess of Kirkcaldy always smiling
And arriving late for tea.
The duke was having problems
With a message at the local bird and bee.
Cry baby cry.
Make your mother sigh.
She's old enough to know better. So cry baby cry.
At twelve o'clock a meeting round the table
For a seance in the dark.
With voices out of nowhere
Put on specially by the children for a lark.
Cry baby cry.
Make your mother sigh.
She's old enough to know better.
So cry baby cry cry cry cry baby.
Make your mother sigh.
She's old enough to know better.
Cry baby cry cry cry cry
Make your mother sigh.
She's old enough to know better.
So cry baby cry.

“Jetzt ist alles aus.
Das ist irgendwie das
Ende, nicht wahr?”
**Diane Robbins,
Teenager aus London,
an dem Tag, als Paul
heiratete**

Good night

Now it's time to say good night
Good night sleep tight.
Now the sun turns out his light
Good night sleep tight.
Dream sweet dreams for me
Dream sweet dreams for you.
Close your eyes and I'll close mine
Good night sleep tight.
Now the moon begins to shine
Good night sleep tight.
Dream sweet dreams for me
Dream sweet dreams for you.
Close your eyes and I'll close mine
Good night sleep tight.
Now the sun turns out his light
Good night sleep tight.
Dream sweet dreams for me.
Dream sweet dreams for you.
Good night good night everybody
Everybody everywhere.
Good night.

All Together Now

One, two, three, four,
Can I have a little more,
Five, six, seven, eight, nine, ten,
I love you.
A, B, C, D,
Can I bring my friend to tea,
E, F, G, H, I, J,
I love you.
Bom bom bom bom-pa bom
Sail the ship bom-pa bom
Chop the tree bom-pa bom
Skip the rope bom-pa bom
Look at me.
All together now, All together now,
All together now, All together now,
Black, white, green, red,
Can I take my friend to bed,
Pink, brown, yellow, orange and blue,
I love you.
All together now, All together now,
All together now, All together now,
Bom bom bom bom bom-pa bom
Sail the ship bom-pa bom
Chop the tree bom-pa bom
Skip the rope bom-pa bom
Look at me
All together now, All together now,
All together now, All together now,
All together now!

Only a Northern Song

If you're listening to this song
You may think the chords are going wrong
But they're not; we just wrote them like that
When you're listening late at night
You may think the band are not quite right
But they are, they just play it like that
It doesn't really matter what chords I play
What words I say or time of day it is
As it's only a Northern song
It doesn't really matter what clothes I wear
Or how I fare or if my hair is brown
When it's only a Northern song.
If you think the harmony
Is a little dark and out of key
You're correct, there's nobody there.
And I told you there's no one there.

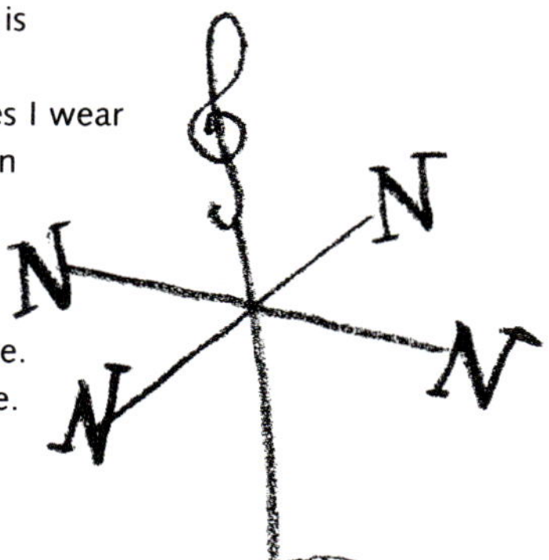

❝Die Sache ist die: Wir sind eigentlich ein und dieselbe Person. Wir sind die vier Teile der einen.❞
Paul

Hey bulldog

Sheep dog standing in the rain.
Bull frog doing it again.
Some kind of happiness is measured out in miles.
What makes you think you're something
special when you smile.
Child-like yeah, no one understands.
Jack-knife in your sweaty hands.
Some kind of innocence is measured out in years.
You don't know what it's like to listen to your fears.
You can talk to me,
You can talk to me,
You can talk to me,
If you're lonely you can talk to me (yeah!)
Big man walking in the park
Wigwam frightened of the dark
Some kind of solitude is measured out in you.
You think you know it but you haven't got a clue.
You can talk to me,
You can talk to me,
You can talk to me,
If you're lonely you can talk to me (yeah!)
Hey bulldog, hey bulldog, hey bulldog
Hey, bulldog, Woof!
Wha'd'ya say?
I said woof!
d'y'know any more?
Wowu-wa Ah!

“Paul sagte, wir sollten im Studio gleich ein richtiges Lied machen und keine Zeit mehr vertrödeln. Ob ich nicht schnell was hinschreiben könnte? Ich hatte ein paar Zeilen zu Hause, die hab ich dann mit ins Studio gebracht.”
John

It’s all too much

It’s all too much
It’s all too much
When I look into your eyes
Your love is there for me
And the more I go inside
The more there is to see.
It’s all too much for me to take
The love that’s shining all around you
Everywhere it’s what you make
for us to take it’s all too much.
Floating down the stream of time
From life to life with me
Makes no difference where you are
or where you’d like to be.
It’s all too much for me to take
The love that’s shining all around here.
All the world is birthday cake
so take a piece but not too much.
Sail me on a silver sun
Where I know that I am free
Show me that I’m everywhere
and get me home for tea.
It’s all too much for me to take
There’s plenty there for everybody
The more you give the more you get
The more it is and it’s too much.
It’s all too much for me to see
The love that’s shining all around you
The more I learn the less I know
But what I do is all too much.
It’s all too much for me to take
The love that’s shining all around you
Everywhere it’s what you make
for us to take it’s all too much.
It’s much, it’s much.
It’s too much
Ah! it’s too much
You are too much ah!
We are dead ah!
Too much, too much, too much-a-FADE

“George schreibt neuerdings sentimentale Lieder, als hätte er Seelen-Durchfall.”
John

Goodbye

Please don't wake me until late tomorrow comes,
And I will not be late.
Late today when it becomes tomorrow.
I will leave to go away.
Goodbye, goodbye, goodbye, goodbye my love
goodbye.
Songs that lingered on my lips excite me now
And linger on my mind.
Leave your flowers at my door
I'll leave them for the one who waits behind.
Far away my lover sings a lonely song
And calls me to his side.
When the song of lonely love
Invites me on I must go to his side.
Goodbye, goodbye, goodbye, goodbye my love
goodbye.

Released by Mary Hopkin, April 1969

›Ich trete nicht länger als der dressierte Floh auf. Ich habe bisher die Träume gesponnen und ich mache auch weiter. Aber ich werde nicht mehr mit 30.000 Stundenkilometern herumrasen, nur um mich selbst zu beweisen. Ich will doch nicht mit 40 schon sterben.‹
John

›Ich hatte nie einen Vertrag mit den Beatles. Ich hatte ihnen gesagt, was ich vorhatte, und versprochen, es durchzuboxen. Das genügte. Ich hielt mich an die Abmachungen, und kein Mensch machte sich Gedanken darüber, ob ich unterschrieben hatte oder nicht.‹
Brian Epstein

Don't let me down

Don't let me down
Don't let me down
Don't let me down
Don't let me down
Nobody ever loved me like she does
Ooh she does. Yes she does
And if somebody loved me
Like she do to me
Ooh she do me. Yes she does
Don't let me down
Don't let me down
Don't let me down
Don't let me down
I'm in love for the first time
Don't you know it's going to last
It's a love that lasts forever
It's a love that has no past
Don't let me down
Don't let me down
Don't let me down
Don't let me down
And from the first time that she really done me
Ooh she done me. She done me good
I guess nobody ever really done me
Ooh she done me
She done me good
Don't let me down
Don't let me down
Don't let me down
Don't let me down

The ballad of John and Yoko

Standing in the dock at Southampton,
Trying to get to Holland or France.
The man in the mac said you've got to go back,
You know they didn't even give us a chance.
Christ! You know it ain't easy,
You know how hard it can be.
The way things are going,
They're going to crucify me.
Finally made the plane into Paris,
Honeymooning down by the Seine.
Peter Brown called to say,
You can make it OK,
You can get married in Gibraltar near Spain.
Christ! You know it ain't easy,
You know how hard it can be.
The way things are going,
They're going to crucify me.
Drove from Paris to the Amsterdam Hilton,
Talking in our beds for a week.
The newspapers said, say what're you doing in bed,
I said we're only trying to get us some peace.
Christ! You know it ain't easy,
You know how hard it can be.
The way things are going,
They're going to crucify me.
Saving up your money for a rainy day,
Giving all your clothes to charity.
Last night the wife said,
Oh boy, when you're dead you don't take
nothing with you but your soul –
Think!
Made a lightning trip to Vienna,
Eating choc'late cake in a bag.
The newspapers said,
She's gone to his head,
They look just like two Gurus in drag.
Christ! You know it ain't easy,
You know how hard it can be.
The way things are going,
They're going to crucify me.
Caught the early plane back to London,
Fifty acorns tied in a sack.
The men from the press said we wish you success,
It's good to have the both of you back.
Christ! You know it ain't easy,
You know how hard it can be.
The way things are going,
They're going to crucify me.

❛ Natürlich bin ich nicht einsam. Ich bin doch Tag und Nacht mit Yoko zusammen. Vielleicht bin ich einsam im philosophischen Sinne, aber es gibt keine Wünsche, die sich auf die Außenwelt richten. Wir sind das Beste, was jedem von uns passieren kann. ❜

John

Give peace a chance

Two one two three four
Ev'rybody's talking about
Bagism, Shagism, Dragism, Madism,
Ragism, Tagism,
This-ism, That-ism, Is-m is-m is-m.
All we are saying is give peace a chance,
All we are saying is give peace a chance.
C'mon.
Ev'rybody's talking about Ministers, Sinisters,
Banisters
And canisters, Bishops, and Fishops,
Rabbis and Pop eyes, Bye bye, bye byes.
All we are saying is give peace a chance,
All we are saying is give peace a chance.
Let me tell you now
Revolution, Evolution, mastication, flagellation,
regulations, integrations,
meditations, United Nations,
Congratulations.
Oh let's stick to it,
John and Yoko, Timmy Leary, Rosemary,
Tommy Smothers, Bobby Dylan, Tommy Cooper,
Derek Taylor, Norman Mailer, Alan Ginsberg,
Hare Krishna, Hare Krishna.

Released by Plastic Ono Band, July 1969

›Auf der Platte habe ich ›masturbation‹ gesungen, aber ich hatte sowieso gerade Ärger wegen der Ballade von ›John und Yoko‹ und wollte nicht noch mehr Krach, deshalb habe ich in der Druckfassung ›mastication‹ geschrieben. Das war natürlich ein Rückzieher, aber die Sache mit dem Frieden war mir wichtiger als der Spaß an einem schmutzigen Wort.‹

John

Come together

He got O-no sideboard
He one spinal cracker
He bag production
He got walrus gumboot
Here come flat top
He come grooving up slowly
He got joo joo eyeball
He one holy roller
He got hair down to his knee.
Got to be a joker he just do what he please.
He wear no shoe shine
He got toe jam football
He got funny finger
He shoot Coca Cola
He say I know you, you know me.
One thing I can tell you is you got to be free.
Come together right now over me.
Come together.
He got feet down below his knee.
Hold you in his armchair you can feel his disease.
Come together right now over me.
Come together.
He roller coaster
He got early warning
He got muddy water
He one Mojo filter
He say one and one and one is three.
Got to be goodlooking 'cos he's so hard to see.
Come together right now over me.
Come together.

›Das sollte erst ein Lied sein für unsere Kampagne, aber dann hat es sich anders entwickelt. Die Leute fragen oft, wie ich schreibe. Nun, das ist immer verschieden. Mal am Klavier, mal mit der Gitarre, in allen Kombinationen. Leicht ist es nicht.‹

John

❛Das ist eine Zusammenfassung der Pleiten, die man im Leben so durchmacht. Kaum, dass die Sache mal glatt geht, kommt schon Maxwells silbernes Hämmerchen runter und macht wieder alles kaputt.❜
Paul

Maxwell's silver hammer

Joan was quizzical studied paraphysical
science in the home
Late night all alone with a test-tube,
oh oh, oh oh.
Maxwell Edison majoring in medicine calls
her on the phone,
Can I take you out to the pictures Joan.
But as she's getting ready to go, a knock
came on the door.
Bang bang Maxwell's silver hammer came
down upon her head,
Bang bang Maxwell's silver hammer made
sure that she was dead.
Back in school again, Maxwell plays the
fool again, teacher gets annoyed,
Wishing to avoid an unpleasant scene,
She tells Max to stay when the class has gone away,
So he waits behind,
Writing fifty times I must not be so
But when she turns her back on the boy,
he creeps up from behind,
Bang bang Maxwell's silver hammer came
down upon her head,
Bang bang Maxwell's silver hammer made
sure that she was dead.
P.C. thirty-one said, we've caught a dirty one,
Maxwell stands alone
Painting testimonial pictures oh oh oh oh
Rose and Valerie screaming from the gallery
say he must go free.
The judge does not agree and he tells them so oh oh.
But as the words are leaving his lips, a
noise comes from behind,
Bang bang Maxwell's silver hammer came
down upon his head,
Bang bang Maxwell's silver hammer made
sure that he was dead.
Silver hammer man.

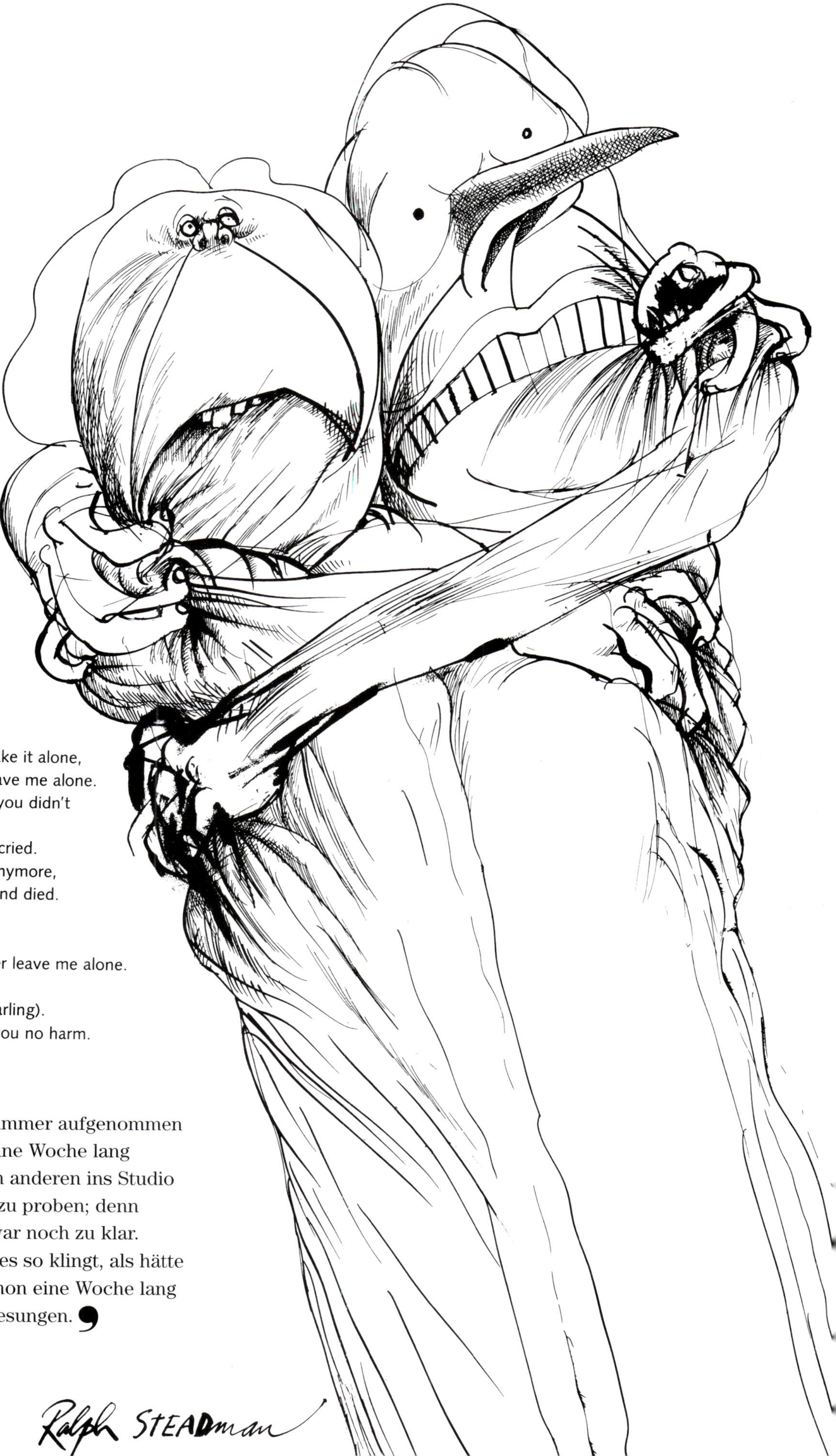

Oh! darling

Oh darling please believe me,
I'll never do you no harm,
Oh! darling, if you leave me I'll never make it alone,
Believe me when I beg you don't ever leave me alone.
(Believe me darling). When you told me you didn't
need me anymore,
Well you know I nearly broke down and cried.
When you told me you didn't need me anymore,
Oh well you know I nearly broke down and died.
Oh! darling, if you leave me,
I'll never make it alone.
Believe me when I tell you, you don't ever leave me alone.
Oh! darling please believe me,
I'll never let you down (Oh believe me darling).
Believe me when I tell you, I'll never do you no harm.
I'll never do you no harm.

❛Als wir diese Nummer aufgenommen haben, bin ich eine Woche lang morgens vor den anderen ins Studio gekommen, um zu proben; denn meine Stimme war noch zu klar. Ich wollte, dass es so klingt, als hätte ich den Song schon eine Woche lang auf der Bühne gesungen.❜
Paul

MAP XII.

THE SKY.

Nov. 22, at 10 o'clock.	Dec. 3, at 9¼ o'clock.	Dec. 14, at 8½ o'clock.
Nov. 25, at 9¾ o'clock.	Dec. 7, at 9 o'clock.	Dec. 17, at 8¼ o'clock.
Nov. 29, at 9½ o'clock.	Dec. 10, at 8¾ o'clock.	Dec. 21, at 8 o'clock.

IN THE EVENING.

Because

Because the world is round it turns me on.
Because the world is round – Ah – love is old,
love is new,
Love is all, love is you.
Because the wind is high it blows my mind.
Because the wind is high – Ah – love is old,
love is new,
Love is all, love is you.
Because the sky is blue it makes me cry.
Because the sky is blue – Ah – love is old,
love is new,
Love is all, love is you.

»Dieses Lied erzählt, wie es am Anfang mit Yoko und mir war. Yoko spielte ein paar Akkorde von Beethoven, und ich sagte: ›Spiel sie doch einmal rückwärts.‹ Eigentlich ist es die Mondschein-Sonate von hinten.«
John

I want you

I want you
I want you so bad
I want you,
I want you so bad
it's driving me mad, it's driving me mad.
I want you
I want you so bad babe
I want you,
I want you so bad
It's driving me mad, it's driving me mad.
Yeah.
I want you
I want you so bad babe
I want you,
I want you so bad
It's driving me mad, it's driving me mad.
I want you
I want you so bad
I want you,
I want you so bad
It's driving me mad, it's driving me mad.
Yeah.
She's so heavy heavy.

»Das Mädchen ist Yoko. Sie ist ziemlich ernsthaft, und ich wusste nichts anderes zu sagen: ›Ich mag dich‹ und ›sie ist so ernsthaft‹. Natürlich sagte jemand, der Text wäre nicht so besonders, aber ich wollte nun mal gar nichts anderes sagen.«
John

Sun king

Ah – here comes the Sun king.
Ev'rybody's laughing,
Ev'rybody's happy.
Here comes the Sun king.
Quando paramucho mi amore defelice corazon
Mundo pararazzi mi amore chicka ferdy parasol
Cuesto obrigado tanta mucho que can eat it carousel.

»Die Beatles selbst sind gar nicht so reich, wie viele Leute wohl annehmen. Gott hat bei der Schöpfung wohl nicht an grüne Äpfel gedacht. Die Verwertungsgesellschaften der Beatles allerdings haben es in sich. Persönlich haben sie gar nicht so viel Geld, wie sie sollten.«
Allen Klein

You never give me your money

You never give me your money
You only give me your funny paper
And in the middle of negotiations you break down
I never give you my number
I only give my situation
And in the middle of investigation I break down.
Out of college money spent
See no future pay no rent.
All the money's gone, nowhere to go.
Any Jobber got the sack,
Monday morning turning back.
Yellow lorry slow, nowhere to go.
But oh – that magic feeling nowhere to go.
One sweet dream
Pick up the bags and get in the limousine.
Soon we'll be away from here.
Step on the gas and wipe that tear away,
One sweet dream came true today, came true today.
One, two, three, four, five, six, seven,
All good children go to heaven.

»Das habe ich geschrieben, als wir all diese finanziellen Schwierigkeiten hatten bei Apple.«
Paul

Pepper

Mean Mr Mustard

Mean Mister Mustard sleeps in the park,
shaves in the dark
trying to save paper.
Sleeps in a hole in the road
Saving up to buy some clothes.
Keeps a ten bob note up his nose,
Such a mean old man, such a mean old man.
His sister Pam works in a shop,
She never stops, she's a go getter.
Takes him out to look at the Queen,
Only place that he's ever been.
Always shouts out something obscene,
Such a dirty old man, dirty old man.

❛Das ist einer von den Songs, die wir in Indien geschrieben haben.❜
John

Polythene Pam

Well you should see Polythene Pam
She's so goodlooking but she looks like a man.
Well you should see her in drag.
Dressed in her polythene bag.
Yes you should see Polythene Pam – Yeh.
Get a dose of her in jackboots and kilt
She's killer diller when she's dressed to the hilt.
She's the kind of a girl that makes the
News of the World.
Yes you could say that she was attractively built – Yeh.

❛Das habe ich in Indien geschrieben, aber bei der Aufnahme habe ich meinen schönsten Liverpool-Dialekt eingesetzt, denn da geht es um diese aufgetakelte mythische Liverpool-Mieze mit Stiefeln und Minirock.❜
John

She came in through the bathroom window

»Das ist ein Teil von einem Medley von ungefähr 15 Minuten, den wir auf ›Abbey Road‹ untergebracht haben. Sowohl John als auch ich hatten eine Reihe angefangener Lieder, die alle ganz großartig waren, aber nie zu Ende geschrieben wurden.«
Paul

Oh look out
She came in through the bathroom window,
Protected by a silver spoon
But now she sucks her thumb and wonders
by the banks of her own lagoon
Didn't anybody tell her
Didn't anybody see
Sundays on the phone to Monday
Tuesdays on the phone to me.
She said she'd always been a dancer
She worked at fifteen clubs a day
And though she thought I knew the answer
Well I knew I could not say.
And so I quit the police department
And got myself a steady job
And though she tried her best to help me
She could steal but she could not rob.

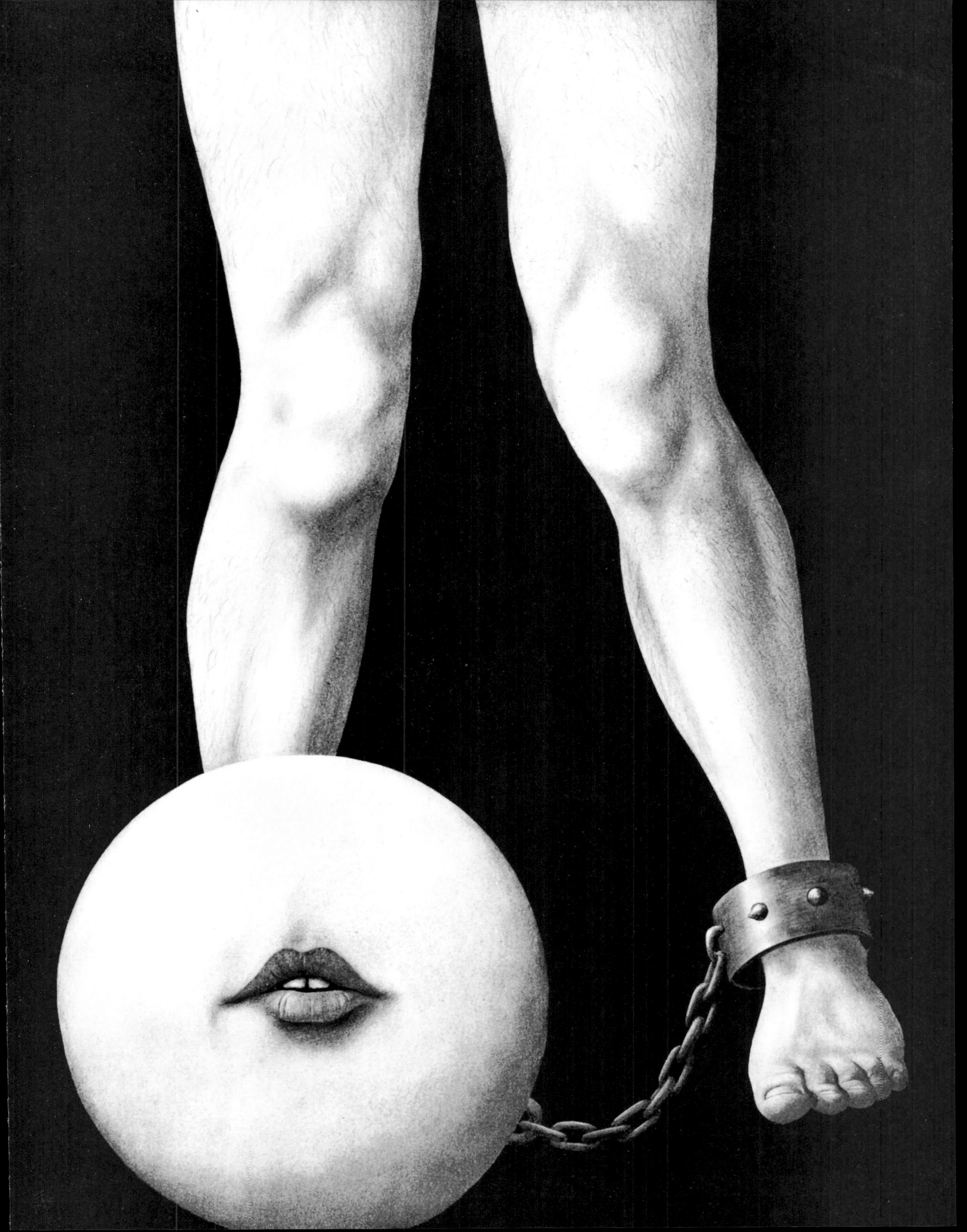

Golden slumbers

Once there was a way to get back homeward.
Once there was a way to get back home.
Sleep pretty darling do not cry,
And I will sing a lullaby.
Golden Slumbers fill your eyes,
Smiles awake you when you rise.
Sleep pretty darling do not cry,
And I will sing a lullaby.

❛Als ich im Haus meines Vaters in Cheshire auf dem Klavier herumklimperte, entdeckte ich in einem Liederbuch meiner Stiefschwester Ruth dieses Lied und dachte, es wäre hübsch, ein eigenes Schlafliedchen zu schreiben.❜
Paul

Carry that weight

Boy – you're gonna carry that weight,
Carry that weight a long time.
I never give you my pillow,
I only send you my invitations,
And in the middle of the celebrations
I break down.

❛Nur in England werden die Beatles gehasst.❜
George

The end

Oh yeah alright, are you gonna be in my dreams
tonight.
And in the end the love you take is equal to the love
you make.
Ah –

»Nicht ich habe die Beatles verlassen, sondern die Beatles haben die Beatles verlassen. Aber keiner will derjenige sein, der den anderen erklärt, dass die Party vorbei ist.«
Paul

END

Her Majesty

Her Majesty's a pretty nice girl but she
doesn't have a lot to say.
Her Majesty's a pretty nice girl but she
changes from day to day.
I wanna tell her that I love her a lot,
but I gotta get a belly full of wine.
Her Majesty's a pretty nice girl,
Someday I'm gonna make her mine – oh yeah,
Someday I'm gonna make her mine.

❛Das Einzige, was ich beim M.B.E. bedauert habe, war allenfalls, dass wir ihn überhaupt angenommen haben. Das war doch glatter Verrat. Wen man bei Hofe gewusst hätte, was ich über das Königshaus denke, hätten wir den Orden sowieso nie gekriegt.❜
John

Cold turkey

Temperature's rising
Fever is high
Can't see no future
Can't see no sky.
My feet are so heavy
So is my head
I wish I was a baby
I wish I was dead.
Cold turkey has got me on the run.
Body is aching
Goose-pimple bone
Can't see no body
Leave me alone.
My eyes are wide open
Can't get to sleep
One thing I'm sure of
I'm in at the deep freeze.
Cold turkey has got me on the run.
Cold turkey has got me on the run.
Thirty six hours
Rolling in pain
Praying to someone
Free me again.
Oh I'll be a good boy
Please make me well
I promise you anything
Get me out of this hell.
Cold turkey has got me on the run.

Released by Plastic Ono Band, October 1969

»Da geht es um Drogenentzug und was man dabei aushalten muss.«
John

Come and get it

If you want it, here it is,
Come and get it,
Make your mind up fast,
If you want it any time
I can give it
But you better hurry 'cos it may not last.
Did I hear you say that there must be a catch
Will you walk away from a fool and his money?
If you want it, here it is,
Come and get it
But you better hurry 'cos it's going fast.
Sonny if you want it, here it is,
Come and get it,
But you better hurry 'cos it's going fast.
You'd better hurry 'cos it's going fast –
Do –.

Released by Badfinger, December 1969

❛Paul sagte mir, er hätte für den Film ›The Magic Christian‹ einen Song geschrieben, und wenn sie sich genau an seine Vorstellung hielten, könnten ihn Badfinger aufnehmen.❜
Bill Collins, Manager von Badfinger

You know my name

You know my name
Look up the number
You know my name
Look up the number
You you know you know my name
You you know you know my name
Good evening and welcome to Slaggers
featuring Denis O'Bell
Come on Ringo let's hear it for Denis
Good evening
You know my name
Better look up my number
You know my name
(That's right) look up my number
You you know you know my name
You you know you know my name
You know my name
Ba ba ba ba ba ba ba ba ba
Look up my number
You know my name
That's right look up the number
Oh you know you know
You know my name you know you know you know my name
Huh huh huh huh
You know my name
Ba ba ba pum
Look up the number
You know my name
Look up the number
You-a you know you know my name
Baby you-a you know you know my name
You know you know my name you know you know my name
Go on Denis let's hear it for Denis O'Bell
You know you know you know my name you know you know
you know my name
Prrr you know my name and the number
You know my name and the number you know you know my
name
Look up the number
You know my number three you know my number two
You know my number three you know my number four
You know my name you know my number too
You know my name you know my number
What's up with you?
You know my name
That's right
Yeah

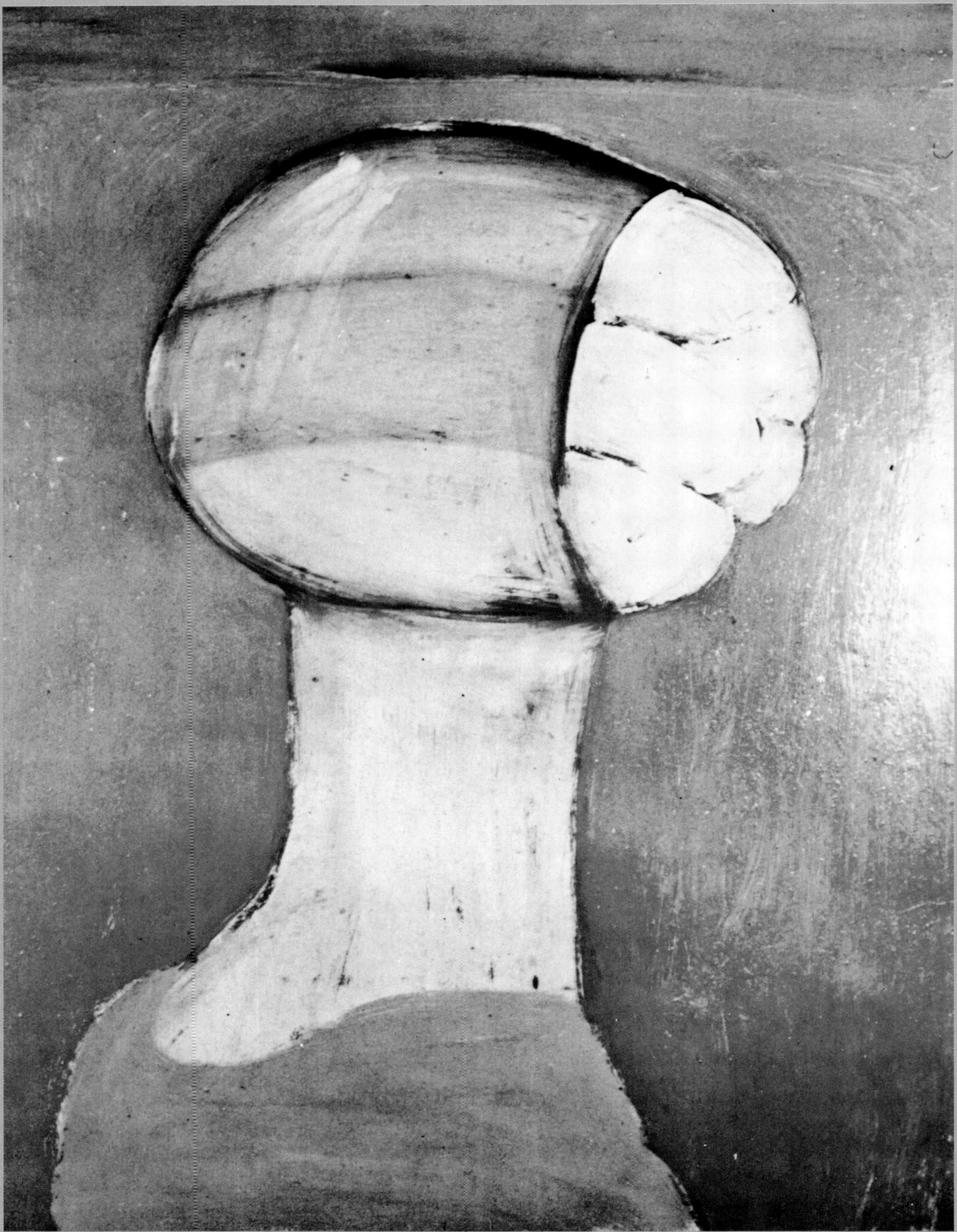

Two of us

Two of us riding nowhere
Spending someone's hard earned pay.
You and me Sunday driving,
Not arriving on our way back home.
We're on our way home,
We're on our way home,
We're going home.
You and I have memories
Longer than the road that stretches out ahead.
Two of us sending postcards
Writing letters on my wall.
You and me burning matches,
Lifting latches on our way back home.
We're on our way home,
We're on our way home,
We're going home.
Two of us wearing raincoats
Standing solo in the sun.
You and me chasing paper,
Getting nowhere on our way back home.
We're on our way home,
We're on our way home,
We're going home.

›Ich habe eine großartige Frau, die ich heute noch mehr liebe als damals, als ich sie geheiratet habe. Ich habe zwei großartige Kinder und ein hübsches Haus. Das alles ist mir sehr kostbar.‹
Paul

Dig a pony

I dig a pony
Well you can celebrate anything you want
Yes you can celebrate anything you want
Ooh.
I do a road hog
Well you can penetrate any place you go,
Yes you can penetrate any place you go
I told you so, all I want is you.
Ev'rything has got to be just like you want it to.
Because –
I pick a moon dog
Well you can radiate ev'rything you are
Yes you can radiate ev'rything you are –
Ooh.
I roll a stoney
Well you can imitate ev'ryone you know
Yes you can imitate ev'ryone you know.
I told you so, all I want is you.
Ev'rything has got to be just like you want it to.
Because –
I feel the wind blow
Well you can indicate ev'rything you see
Yes you can indicate ev'rything you see –
Ooh.
I dug a pony
Well you can syndicate any boat you row
Yes you can syndicate any boat you row.
I told you so, all I want is you.
Ev'rything has got to be just like you want it to.
Because –

„Bei der Arbeit im Studio konnten wir die Songs einen nach dem anderen entstehen lassen."
George Martin, Producer der Beatles

Across the universe

Words are flying out like endless rain into a paper cup,
They slither while, they pass, they slip away across the universe.
Pools of sorrow, waves of joy are drifting through my open mind,
possessing and caressing me.
Jai Guru De Va Om
Nothing's gonna change my world
Nothing's gonna change my world.
Images of broken light which dance before me like a million eyes,
That call me on and on across the universe,
Thoughts meander like a restless wind
inside a letter box they
tumble blindly as they make their way
across the universe
Jai Guru De Va Om
Nothing's gonna change my world
Nothing's gonna change my world.
Sounds of laughter shades of earth are ringing
through my open views inciting and inviting me.
Limitless undying love which shines around me like a million suns, it calls me on and on across the universe
Jai Guru De Va Om
Nothing's gonna change my world
Nothing's gonna change my world.

❛Das war einer meiner Lieblingssongs, aber er ist in so vielen Fassungen veröffentlicht worden, dass er es nie richtig geschafft hat. Erst habe ich ihn dem World Wild Life Fund geschenkt, aber die wussten nichts Rechtes damit anzufangen, deshalb haben wir ihn dann auf das Let It Be-Album getan.❜
John

Dig it

Like a rolling stone
A like a rolling stone
Like the FBI and the CIA
And the BBC ... BB King,
And Doris Day.
Matt Busby.
Dig it, dig it, dig it,
Dig it, dig it, dig it, dig it, dig it, dig it, dig it, dig it.

❛Das habe ich so an Ort und Stelle aus dem Ärmel geschüttelt. So klingt's auch? Ja, finde ich auch.❜
John

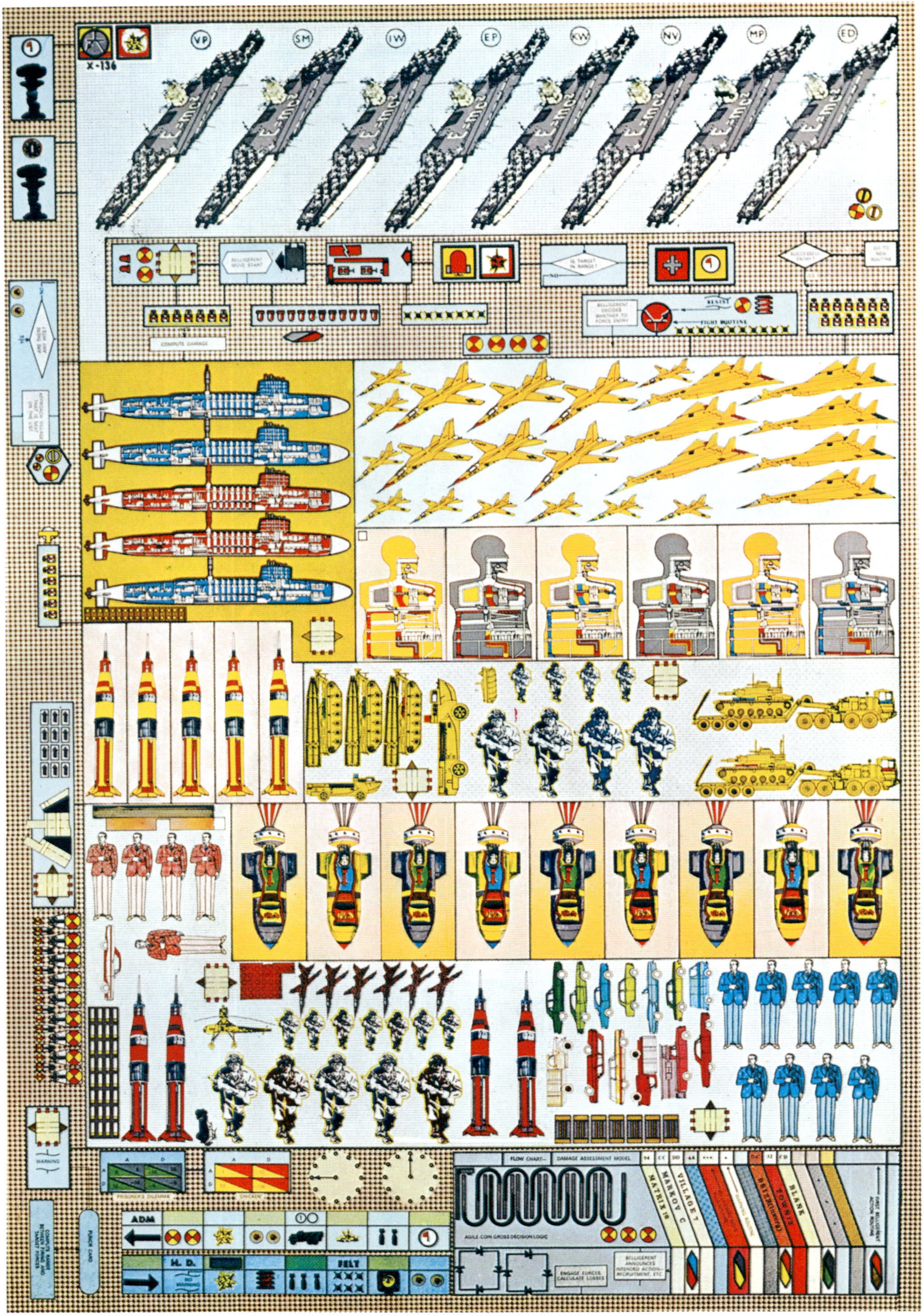
X-136
VP
SM
IW
EP
KW
NV
MP
ED
BELLIGERENT MOVE START
IS TARGET IN RANGE?
NO
SUCCESSFUL ENTRY?
GO TO NEW ROUTINE
BELLIGERENT DECIDES WHETHER TO FORCE ENTRY
RESIST
FIGHT ROUTINE
COMPUTE DAMAGE
WARNING
ADM
H. D.
FELT
FLOW CHART—
DAMAGE ASSESSMENT MODEL
MATRIX 18
MARKOV C
VILLAGE 7
TOWN 12
BLANK
FIRST BELLIGERENT ACTION ROUTINE
AGILE-COIN GROSS DECISION LOGIC
ENGAGE FORCES CALCULATE LOSSES
BELLIGERENT ANNOUNCES INTENDED ACTION— RECRUITMENT, ETC

I've got a feeling

I've got a feeling, a feeling deep inside
Oh yeah, Oh yeah.
I've got a feeling, a feeling I can't hide
Oh no, Oh no, Oh no,
Yeah I've got a feeling.
On please believe me
I'd hate to miss the train
Oh yeah, Oh yeah.
And if you leave me I won't be late again
Oh no, Oh no, Oh no.
Yeah I've got a feeling yeah.
All these years I've been wandering around,
wondering how come nobody told me
All that I was looking for was somebody
who looked like you.
Ev'rybody had a hard year
Ev'rybody had a good time
Ev'rybody had a wet dream,
Ev'rybody saw the sunshine
Oh yeah, Oh yeah, Oh yeah.
Ev'rybody had a good year,
Ev'rybody let their hair down,
Ev'rybody pulled their socks up,
Ev'rybody put their foot down.
Oh yeah, Oh yeah, Oh yeah.

Let it be

When I find myself in times of trouble
Mother Mary comes to me
Speaking words of wisdom, let it be.
And in my hour of darkness
She is standing right in front of me
Speaking words of wisdom, let it be.
Let it be, let it be.
Whisper words of wisdom, let it be.
And when the broken hearted people
Living in the world agree,
There will be an answer, let it be.
For though they may be parted there is
Still a chance that they will see
There will be an answer, let it be.
Let it be, let it be. Yeah
There will be an answer, let it be.
And when the night is cloudy,
There is still a light that shines on me,
Shine until tomorrow, let it be.
I wake up to the sound of music,
Mother Mary comes to me,
Speaking words of wisdom, let it be.
Let it be, let it be.
There will be an answer, let it be.
Let it be, let it be,
Whisper words of wisdom, let it be.

One after 909

My baby says she's trav'ling on the One after
Nine-O-Nine,
I said move over honey I'm travelling on that line.
I said move over once, move over twice,
Come on baby don't be cold as ice.
I said I'm trav'ling on the One after Nine-O-Nine.
I begged her not to go and I begged her on
my bended knees,
You're only fooling around, you're fooling
around with me.
I said move over once, move over twice,
Come on baby don't be cold as ice.
I said I'm trav'ling on the One after Nine-O-Nine.
I've got my bag,
run to the station.
Railman says you've got the wrong location.
I've got my bag,
run right home.
Then I find I've got the number wrong,
Well I said I'm trav'ling on the One after
Nine-O-Nine.
I said move over honey I'm travelling on that line.
I said move over once, move over twice,
Come on baby don't be cold as ice.
I said we're trav'ling on the One after
Nine-O,
I said we're trav'ling on the One after
Nine-O,
I said we're trav'ling on the One after
Nine-O-Nine.

"Das ist eins der ersten Lieder, das ich je geschrieben habe, für den Film Let It Be haben wir es dann wiederbelebt."
John

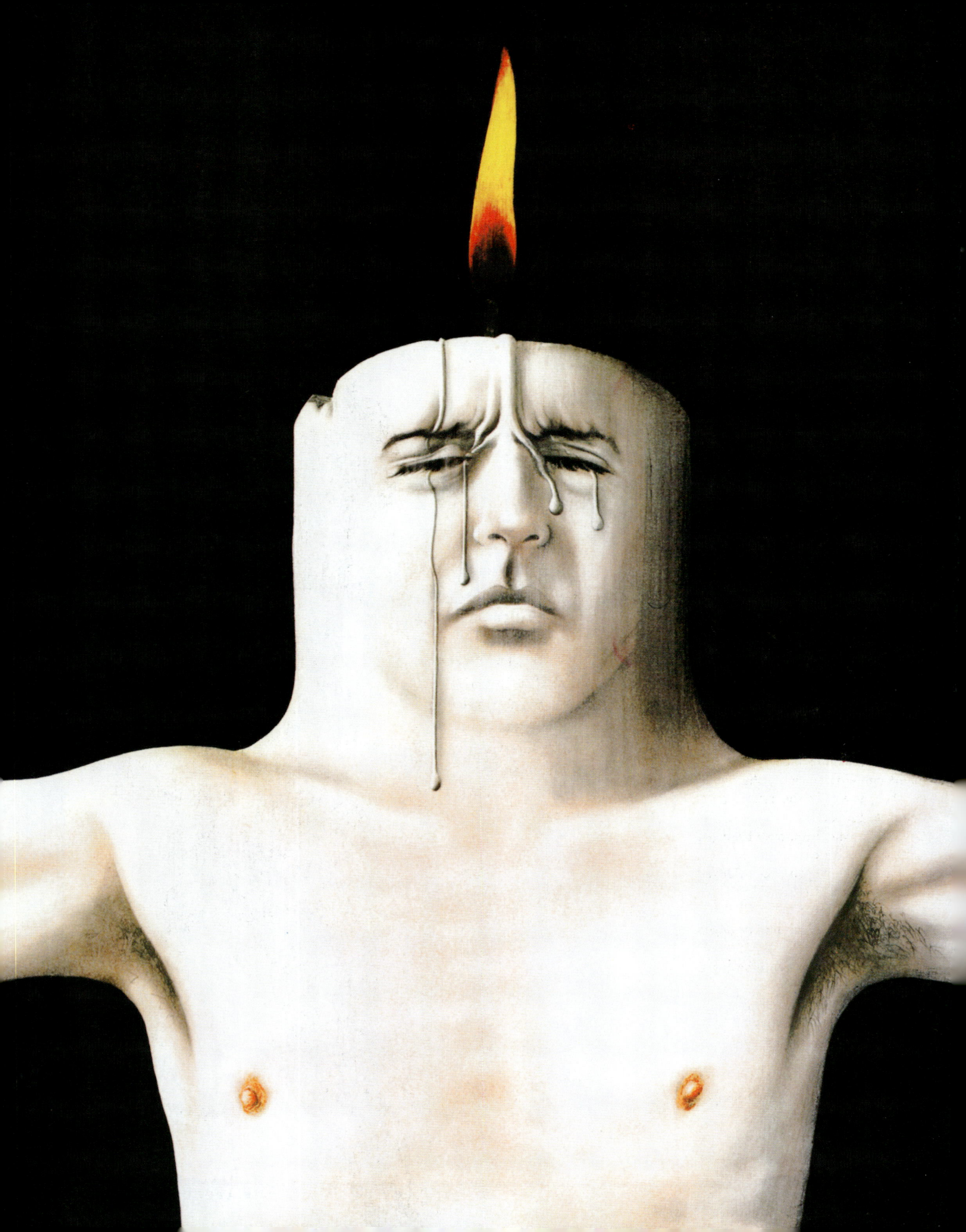

The long and winding road

The long and winding road that leads to your door,
Will never disappear, I've seen that road before
It always leads me here, leads me to your door.
The wild and windy night that the rain washed away,
Has left a pool of tears crying for the day.
Why leave me standing here, let me know the way.
Many times I've been alone and many times I've cried,
Anyway you'll never know the many ways I've tried, but
Still they lead me back to the long and winding road,
You left me standing here a long, long time ago.
Don't leave me waiting here, lead me to your door.
Da da, da da –

Get back

(1)
Jojo was a man who thought he was a loner
But he knew it couldn't last.
Jojo left his home in Tucsan, Arizona
For some California Grass.
Get back, get back.
Get back to where you once belonged
Get back, get back.
Get back to where you once belonged.
Get back Jojo. Go home
Get back, get back.
Back to where you once belonged
Get back, get back.
Back to where you once belonged.
Get back Jo.
(2)
Sweet Loretta Martin thought she was a woman
But she was another man
All the girls around her say she's got it coming
But she gets it while she can.
Get back, get back.
Get back to where you once belonged
Get back, get back.
Get back to where you once belonged.
Get back Loretta. Go home
Get back, get back.
Get back to where you once belonged
Get back, get back.
Get back to where you once belonged.
Get back Loretta
Your mother's waiting for you
Wearing her high-heel shoes
And her low-neck sweater
Get on home Loretta
Get back, get back.
Get back to where you once belonged.

❛Wir saßen im Studio und griffen das so aus der Luft. Auch der Text wurde gleich an Ort und Stelle geschrieben. Als wir fertig waren, haben wir es bei Apple aufgenommen, und es wurde ein Lied zum Achterbahnfahren…❜
Paul

Verzeichnis der Songs mit ihren Illustratoren

Dank

Viele haben an diesem Buch mitgearbeitet. Ganz besonders möchte ich Art Kane danken, der den Ball ins Rollen brachte, und all jenen, die Bilder beisteuerten, ohne dadurch reich zu werden. Dank schulden wir auch den Fans, die unsere Annoncen mit erstaunlichen Leistungen beantworteten: Ken White, Thelma Cowen, Alan Birch, Allan Jones, Frances Platt, G. Dean, Molly Booth, David Wright, Anita Johnson, Carole Smith, Tony Rushton, Doreen Hyde, Joan Langford, Richard Phillips, Shennell Rothman, Terry Hynes, Hilary Petch, Dennis McKeown, Irene Hanson, B. Cawson, L. Baker, Martin Lawson, Stephen McGee, Joanne Thomson, F. Ashcroft, Christine und Pauline Westley, S. McCarthy, Pat Laythorpe, Alan Crawley, Stewart Emmott, S. Hurst, V. McCartney, C. Hanne, P. Stennett, Jan Moller, B. Cohen, Allan Le Carpentier, K. Voels, Kevin Day, Mike Davies, Alan Platt und die vielen anderen. Danken möchten wir auch Ray Connolly, der die Bildunterschriften besorgte. Dem Verlag Heinemann danken wir für die freundliche Genehmigung, Auszüge aus der autorisierten Biografie von Hunter Davies 'The Beatles' wiederzugeben.

Herausgeber

Alan Aldridge, einer der innovativsten Grafik-Designer, war ein enger Freund der Beatles, was zu vielen gemeinsamen Projekten führte. Sein eigenwilliger, unmittelbarer Stil und seine brillante Technik haben zahllose Nachahmer auf den Plan gerufen. Seinen vielfach preisgekrönten Arbeiten begegnet man immer wieder in englischen Zeitschriften, auf Plakatwänden und Plattenhüllen.